NEW ZEALAND
LAND *of* BIRDS

NEW ZEALAND
LAND *of* BIRDS

Geoff Moon

NEW HOLLAND

CONTENTS

PREFACE

New Zealand: Land of Birds aims to illustrate some of New Zealand's birds and the wide variety of environments in which they live, feed and breed. The text encompasses the great diversity of landscapes within this country, from sand and surf to rock and snow. Including offshore islands, open sea, shorelines and estuaries, the chapters also take the reader through wetlands and forests to the high country and mountains, as well as to the countryside and urban settlements.

The species of birds presented is a selective one, chosen with the aim of highlighting the relationships that exist between the birds and their environments. Some birds are familiar, some less well known, but all interact with the places they inhabit and the other living creatures around them. Some birds are numerous, others face a battle for survival from introduced predators and, frequently, the modification of their habitats. They are all part of the rich diversity of life in New Zealand, and play an important part in its natural heritage. I hope that this book will contribute to a greater understanding and enjoyment of this land and its birdlife.

It is not the intention of the book to provide complete information on all bird species inhabiting New Zealand, and a field guide should be consulted for this purpose.

All illustrations have been reproduced from transparencies taken in New Zealand. None of these has been altered or enhanced by digital manipulation.

In conclusion, I would like to acknowledge the numerous people who have helped me with advice, or provided opportunities to photograph the many subjects illustrating this book.

Special thanks must go to my wife Lynnette, for her involvement in the book, particularly for the considerable time spent in helping with the text.

I also wish to thank Ray Richards for his encouragement in presenting this book to an enthusiastic publisher, to Renée Lang for her keen interest, Barbara Nielsen for work with the design and Brian O'Flaherty for editing the manuscript.

Geoff Moon
Titirangi, Auckland
2001

INTRODUCTION

NEW ZEALAND – A PRISTINE WILDERNESS

New Zealand once formed a small corner of the ancient supercontinent of Gondwanaland, along with Australia, India, South America, Africa and Antarctica. Around 80 million years ago, as the supercontinent gradually broke up and the Tasman Sea widened, the New Zealand landmass became separated from Australia, and today lies some 2000 kilometres distant. Cast adrift in the South Pacific, New Zealand became one of the world's most isolated landmasses of its size.

New Zealand can aptly be called the 'land of birds'. After separation from Gondwanaland, its varied and unique wildlife and plants developed without contact with the rest of the earth. Its fauna consisted only of birds, reptiles and invertebrates. When New Zealand became isolated from the supercontinent, mammals and snakes had not yet invaded the Australian area of Gondwanaland. And it was only later that the two species of bat, New Zealand's only native mammals, arrived. There are still no snakes in New Zealand; it is one of the few temperate countries without them.

The country's isolation meant that New Zealand still has a relatively high proportion of endemic birds, compared with other countries which were more easily colonised by birds from surrounding regions. The lack of mammalian predators resulted in the evolution of many unique species of birds with features such as large size, flightlessness and a slower reproductive rate. It also meant New Zealand has retained birdlife of ancient lineage. Birds which had an ancestry in Gondwanaland may still be found here. An obvious example is the kiwi, the national symbol, which evolved from an ancient group of flightless birds, the ratites.

THE ANCIENT FORESTS

Up to around 800 years ago, primeval forest covered most of the land. In parts of the North Island, forests of the majestic kauri were common, but did not flourish south of 39 degrees latitude. Remnants of these great forests still exist in Northland, Auckland and Coromandel. Mixed broadleaf and podocarp forest extended across the lowland North Island, such as are preserved in the Whirinaki and Pureora forests today. *Nothofagus* beech forest spread over the mountain ranges. Except in the high rainfall areas of the South Island, such as the west coast, beech was the predominant forest cover, and still is in areas such as Fiordland National Park. Alpine vegetation and tussock extended above the bush line and across the high country as it does to this day.

RIGHT: Before the arrival of humans, primeval forest covered much of New Zealand.

PREVIOUS PAGES: South Island pied oystercatchers rest at high tide on a large shellbank at Miranda in the Firth of Thames.

The original primeval forest that once extended over a large part of the central North Island was destroyed by the cataclysmic Taupo eruption around 1800 years ago. Tussock and scrub vegetation soon colonised the pumice layer and this was progressively invaded by some larger tree species, seeded from neighbouring forests which had escaped the volcanic showers.

In this forest-carpeted land, devoid of humans or other mammals, birds roamed freely. The largest bird of prey ever known, the extinct New Zealand eagle, soared over valleys and peaks. The moa, completely wingless, and some up to 3 metres tall, grazed peacefully. The forests, coasts and mountains all teemed with birdlife. Birdsong filled the valleys at dawn and calls echoed through the night.

THE ARRIVAL OF POLYNESIANS

This avian paradise was severely disrupted by the arrival of the first human settlers. Waves of Polynesian seafarers, presumed to have originated in the eastern Pacific islands, and ancestors of Maori, crossed vast expanses of sea to begin arriving in their new land around 800 to 1000 years ago. The consequences of their arrival for New Zealand's birds were catastrophic.

Maori first settled in the east coast regions of both main islands, using fire to clear vegetation and so provide land for cultivating their crops. Sometimes these fires spread uncontrolled and devastated extensive areas of forest. Where the burned land was not used for cultivation, it was soon overtaken by tussock grasses and scrub, a type of vegetation which persists in low rainfall regions, particularly in eastern parts of the South Island.

Birds were a major food source for the Maori settlers. Seabirds like shearwaters, petrels, shags and gulls were harvested in large numbers, often taken as chicks, from offshore island and mainland nests or burrows. Forest birds were snared and speared, and flightless birds were easy prey.

As well as their food plants, Maori introduced two mammals: the kuri, a dog, now extinct, and the kiore, a small Polynesian rat. Unfortunately, the native birds had not developed any facility to defend themselves against these terrestrial predators. The dogs were used for hunting many species of flightless birds, and some undoubtedly escaped into the wild. Besides eliminating the moa, the Maori hunters and their dogs were responsible for the extinction of several other bird species. The kiore is a proficient climber, and will eat eggs as well as chicks. Its introduction is thought to have been greatly destructive to birdlife, as well as exterminating various species of snails, lizards and frogs.

FAR LEFT: Stands of dense podocarp forest still survive west of Lake Taupo and in the Urewera National Park as well as the Raukumara Range in the North Island.

LEFT: Mature *Nothofagus* beech forest in Fiordland.

According to the eminent palaeontologist and ornithologist, the late Sir Charles Fleming, writing in Volume 1 of *New Zealand Nature Heritage*: 'The arrival of Polynesian man in New Zealand, together with his dog and rat and his knowledge of fire, brought about changes in New Zealand ecology more severe than any of the violent fluctuations of climate that had taken place since the first ice age some 1,750,000 years ago.'

Around 200 years ago, probably about 60 per cent of land below 1000 metres was still forest clad, with tussock and alpine vegetation growing above the tree line. However, almost all the original forest on the east coasts of both main islands had disappeared; only a few areas, such as Banks Peninsula and the Catlins, had escaped destruction. The forests of Stewart Island remained intact.

THE DESTRUCTIVE FORCE OF EUROPEAN SETTLEMENT

The arrival of European settlers in the early nineteenth century had a devastating effect on the New Zealand environment. It was inevitable that they would clear forest to create pastures for farming, but much of this clearance was unnecessarily ruthless, and destruction of much of the native bush from the high country caused rapid rainfall run-off which eroded hillsides and flooded lowland areas. At the same time, the settlers introduced many exotic plants and trees. Some, like gorse, broom, blackberry and wild rose, spread rapidly in the favourable climate and, although many of the exotic deciduous trees brought beauty to the countryside, certain tree species, such as willow, soon began to pose ecological problems.

Introduced browsing animals, notably deer, pigs, goats and Australian brush-tailed possums, caused widespread destruction of native forests. Possums damaged shrubs and canopy trees. They were originally thought to be strict vegetarians, but recent evidence has proved that they are predators of birds' eggs, chicks, and even adult birds. Grazing deer and goats, as well as pigs digging up the forest floor, discouraged regeneration of trees.

Charles Darwin, on a visit to New Zealand in 1835, forecast that the more dominant immigrants, both imported and self-introduced, would result in '...the destruction of the delicate balance of the endemic productions which had reached a standard of perfection attained in long isolation...'

The country's abundant birdlife fell easy prey to the adept climbing ship rats, Norway rats and house mice introduced by European settlers in the late eighteenth and early nineteenth centuries. Further threats were provided by introduced stoats, ferrets and weasels, which had been brought in to control rabbits. Domestic cats, particularly those which had turned feral, also became formidable predators.

LEFT: Much of New Zealand has been transformed into pastoral and arable farmland, environments providing habitats for many bird species.

It is believed that introduced birds, mainly from Europe, brought diseases with them to which native birds had no immunity. The result was that some native bird species, already decimated by predators, were eliminated in some areas such as the Waitakere Ranges.

Besides the destruction of much of New Zealand's native forests, the wetlands and waterways sustained similar damage. Swamps were drained to produce land for agriculture, with resultant loss of their birdlife. This alteration of the environment and disturbance of the natural ecology has continued to the present.

PRESERVATION AND CONSERVATION

Thankfully, in spite of the marked alteration of New Zealand's pristine environment, there are still many areas where birdlife abounds. Reserves and sanctuaries provide refuge for birdlife, and Department of Conservation programmes have contributed greatly to the preservation of species and their habitats. Numerous islands lie off the coast of New Zealand and as a number of these are predator-free, they provide sanctuary for many endangered native birds. While a permit is required to visit some of the sanctuaries, such as Little Barrier Island, there are several which hold no restrictions to visitors. One of these, Tiritiri Matangi, is within easy reach of Auckland. The island is rich in birdlife, and as well as common species, many of the endangered birds now breed there. The larger Kapiti Island, near Wellington, is also home to many rare and endangered species and permits to visit are easily obtained. Stewart Island and many mainland areas, in particular the extensive national parks, retain magnificent forests, lakes and rivers as well as dramatic alpine habitats. These continue to support several species of native birds. As well, much of the country's easily accessible coastline is little changed, still sustaining the sea and coastal birds which frequent it.

In recent years the Department of Conservation has selected certain areas of native forest as special 'islands', where intensive control of predators has resulted in a remarkable increase in the breeding success of many native bird species. The King Country Mapara Forest is one such mainland 'island'. Before predator control commenced, the resident kokako population was only able to rear two or three chicks in a season, but following a few years' control of possums, stoats, cats and rats, more than 50 kokako chicks were being fledged each season, proving beyond doubt the severe impact that predators were having on the native bird population.

TOP: Much of New Zealand's long coastline is home to many species of seabirds.

BOTTOM: Large numbers of migrant waders visit our harbours and estuaries each summer, after nesting in the northern tundra regions.

The benefits of this predator control had a similar positive effect on the breeding success of all other bird species, lizards and invertebrates, as well as resulting in the prolific flowering of native plants.

Another more ambitious project has been the establishment of an 'island' in the heart of Wellington City. A predator-proof fence, over 8 kilometres in length, has been constructed around a native forest and reservoir area in the Karori district. All mammalian predators within the sanctuary have been eliminated, allowing endangered species of birds and reptiles to be introduced.

A recent remarkable event was the release of the endangered little spotted kiwi into the Karori sanctuary, taken from nearby Kapiti Island. This is the first time in 125 years that this smallest species of kiwi has lived on the mainland.

In addition to assistance from conservation programmes, many birds have survived independently, as they have been able to adapt to the ecological changes wrought by human intervention.

BIRDS AND THEIR HABITATS

New Zealand's birdlife consists of the unique land birds, which developed in long isolation, the tube-nosed seabirds, the native and migrant waders, and the many species of introduced passerines (perching birds).

With its position as islands in the Pacific Ocean, New Zealand is a centre of seabird activity, and in particular has a great diversity and very great numbers of tube-nosed seabirds. Wading birds, most migrating from Siberia and Alaska, arrive in large flocks to spend the summer months feeding on the mudflats and estuaries.

New Zealand is geographically diverse and within a comparatively small landmass has a surprising variety of habitats that are home to birds. This book depicts these varying landscapes and the ecological relationships between the many species of birds within them.

Some birds occupy several habitats, one of the most notable being the kingfisher. Favourite haunts are sheltered marine harbours, particularly in winter when insect food is scarce inland. The birds are also attracted to open country and wetlands, as well as forests, especially during nesting when dead trees provide an ideal site for boring a nest tunnel. Black-backed gulls, usually associated with marine habitats, also occur in urban areas and as far inland as the high country. White-faced herons occupy marine habitats but are regularly seen in wetlands and pastures. And Australasian harriers, although choosing to nest in swampland, hunt over wide areas, along coasts, open country and to the foothills of mountain ranges.

Other birds move through one habitat to another, according to seasonal needs and in search of food.

ABOVE: Migrant waders in flight, in the Firth of Thames.

LEFT: Introduced deciduous trees are favoured by many bird species, particularly finches.

A HERITAGE RECLAIMED

Conservationists now have a greater understanding of New Zealand's birdlife, the unique characteristics of the birds and the important niche that they occupy in the ecosystem of each environment. This knowledge contributes to a growing success in protecting birdlife.

It is greatly encouraging that acknowledgement of the urgent need to conserve and enhance the environment is becoming more widespread. Today, New Zealanders increasingly appreciate the fragility of the country's ecosystems and the need to sustain and preserve them. We have come to value the country's precious forest remnants with their diverse plant and animal associations, majestic mountain landscapes and the spectacular and varying coastline where vast stretches of sandy beaches and rocky headlands remain unspoiled. We have come to value too the richness of the country's unique birdlife within these ecosystems.

THE SEA AND OFFSHORE ISLANDS

Sharp rocks drive back the breaking waves,
Confusing sea with air...

– VERNON WATKINS

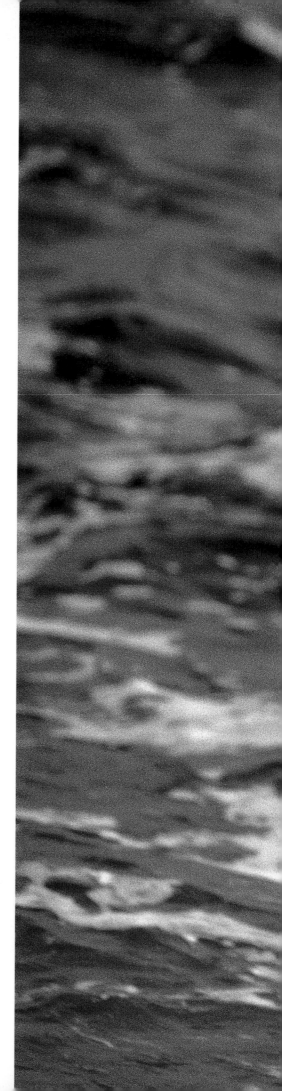

HABITATS OF THE SEA AND OFFSHORE ISLANDS

The seas surrounding New Zealand are probably some of the least modified of this country's diverse landscapes. Compared with those in many other parts of the world, the waters are relatively unpolluted, and their remoteness, with the vast Pacific Ocean stretching away to the east and the Tasman Sea to the west, ensures that they will probably remain this way. However, the marine ecology in some areas is threatened, and in certain parts already is affected to a major degree, especially by over-exploitation by the fishing industry. This could cause a chain reaction, upsetting the natural balance and eventually affecting all marine creatures dependent on the sea for their food.

Offshore islands lie within 50 kilometres of the mainland, while those lying further away than this are termed 'outlying islands'. The oceanic environment dominates the ecology of all these islands and climates tend to be milder than on the mainland. New Zealand's offshore islands extend from the Three Kings group in the far north to the numerous islands which lie close to the coast of Stewart Island in the south.

PREVIOUS PAGES: Codfish Island (Whenua Hou), situated off the north-west coast of Stewart Island, is a predator-free sanctuary, where the main population of the highly endangered kakapo survive.

ABOVE: The endemic Buller's shearwater nests only on the Poor Knights Islands.

RIGHT: Flesh-footed shearwaters are commonly seen in coastal waters. Like the other tube-nosed flesh-footed species of pelagic seabirds, they only come ashore to nest.

Most of the offshore islands were joined to the mainland during the last ice age, and when they became separated, as the sea level rose again with the melting of ice, they still retained the indigenous fauna and flora. Although some islands were later exploited for their timber and some for farming, it was with the introduction of goats, pigs and mammalian predators that birdlife and plants suffered the most. Not only was so much of the forest habitat destroyed, but the introduced animals competed for food and uprooted seedling plants. However, certain islands retained species of fauna and flora which had become extinct on the mainland.

Some outlying islands, such as the Chathams to the east and the Snares and other subantarctic islands, developed their own subspecies of birds in a predator-free environment. These birds would face certain extinction today should rats be inadvertently introduced by visiting boats.

BIRDLIFE OF THE SEA AND OFFSHORE ISLANDS

New Zealand's position in the Pacific, the largest and most productive ocean in the world, as well as its extensive coastline along with numerous offshore and outlying islands, have resulted in the country being endowed with a diversity of seabird species. Half the world's shearwaters and shags are to be found here, and there are numerous representatives of other seabird groups.

ABOVE: The white-faced storm petrel, only 20 centimetres in length, is the smallest of the tube-nosed seabirds.

ABOVE: A northern royal albatross on its nest at Taiaroa Head.

BELOW: The world population of sooty shearwaters is estimated to number over 20 million birds.

Tube-nosed seabirds

By far the commonest of these seabirds are the Procellariiformes, the pelagic tube-noses, distinguished by their tube-shaped nostrils which are positioned externally on the top of the bill. This is the only order of birds composed entirely of marine species, and they are thoroughly adapted to life at sea, only coming ashore to reproduce. Before the arrival of humans and mammalian predators, many tube-nosed species bred on the mainland. Now offshore and outlying islands provide safer sites for them to nest, while a few species still nest on some remote parts of the mainland.

Apart from whales, dolphins and seals, these tube-nosed birds are the only conspicuous wildlife of the open seas. All members of this order are gregarious, and nest in loose colonies. The albatrosses and some petrels choose open ground and the shearwaters and smaller petrels dig burrows or use rock crevices for their nests.

All tube-nose species lay only one egg per clutch, which each parent incubates in turn. Some species, such as Hutton's shearwater and the black Westland petrel, nest on the South Island mainland. Hutton's shearwaters nest in burrows at an altitude above 1500 metres in the Seaward Kaikoura Mountains, and the Westland petrels nest in burrows on the coastal hills near Barrytown in Westland. Grey-faced petrels still nest on some North Island headlands, but many of their earlier colonies have been deserted due to interference by dogs and other predators.

Some of these tube-nosed seabirds exist in vast numbers. The sooty shearwater or muttonbird forms the largest population of any seabird, with a world population estimated to number over 20 million birds. After nesting, dense rafts of these birds can be viewed off the east coasts of New Zealand, on their annual migration north to winter in the subarctic regions of the northern Pacific Ocean. Other species of petrels and shearwaters also migrate to the northern Pacific Ocean after nesting.

The northern royal albatross has managed to maintain a small protected colony at Taiaroa Head on the Otago Peninsula, and also nests on southern outlying islands. The successful breeding of the albatrosses at Taiaroa Head was due entirely to the persistent conservation efforts of the late Dr L.E. Richdale. The species had attempted to nest there from 1920, but human interference and vandalism had frustrated their nesting efforts. However, after strict protection measures were enforced, the birds finally hatched and reared their first chick in 1938. Since then the small protected colony has thrived.

As well as providing safe nesting habitats for the tube-noses and other species such as penguins, shags and gulls, those offshore islands which are free from predators offer sanctuary for several species of endemic land birds, reptiles, invertebrates and plants which once existed on the mainland.

ABOVE: The shy mollymawk nests on several subantarctic islands and the Chathams. They are commonly seen around fishing boats in the waters around Stewart Island.

LEFT: Surprisingly, gannets nest in colonies on the south-west of the active White Island volcano, in the Bay of Plenty. Gannet colonies are shown on the right of the photograph.

ABOVE: A North Island saddleback.

RIGHT: The Hen and Chickens Islands, off the east coast of Northland, were named by Captain Cook. The islands are an important sanctuary for several bird species. Taranga, until 1965, was the only location of the North Island saddleback.

OFFSHORE ISLANDS AND CONSERVATION

Resolution Island lies within Dusky Sound in Fiordland, and is not strictly classed an offshore island. But it is important in the sense that it was the first island to be used in attempted conservation. Richard Henry was the first government-approved ranger stationed in Fiordland and, for 15 years from 1894, he laboured to save the kakapo and kiwi from predation by stoats. He ferried hundreds of kakapo from the mainland to Resolution Island only to find some years later that the stoats were able to swim and again prey upon the birds. These predators finally eliminated the island's kakapo, which Henry described as his 'poor, simple, defenceless and flightless old New Zealanders'.

Taranga, the main island in the Hen and Chickens group of islands in the Hauraki Gulf, is a good example of a predator-free offshore island whose existence prevented a species of endemic bird from becoming extinct. This island was the last remaining home of the North Island saddleback, a wattlebird related to the endangered kokako and extinct huia, and it was once common in mainland forests. In 1966 several saddlebacks were caught and transferred to other predator-free islands where they thrived and bred so successfully that further transfers were made with equal success.

A similar transfer operation was carried out urgently when it was discovered that muttonbirders had inadvertently introduced rats to Big South Cape Island off Stewart Island, and these were decimating the remaining population of the South Island saddleback. The saddlebacks were successfully transferred to safety, but several subspecies of endemic birds, such as the rare snipe and tiny bush wren, were exterminated by the rats. The bush wren is now extinct but a subspecies of the snipe still survives on South East Island in the Chathams and on some subantarctic islands.

Although the transfers of saddlebacks have proved successful, it is unlikely that the species can be introduced to the mainland forests, as the bird frequently feeds on the ground, searching for insects in the forest floor litter. However, they may eventually be introduced to some of the mainland 'islands', mentioned in the Introduction. These sanctuaries are predator-free.

One of New Zealand's most important offshore sanctuaries, and one of world renown, is Hauturu, or Little Barrier Island, in the outer Hauraki Gulf. Covering some 2800 hectares and rising to over 700 metres, the rugged landscape is clothed in dense rainforest. The coastline of the island is precipitous, except for an area in the south-west where a spectacular boulder beach fringes an area of flat land. Because of this, landing on the island is difficult, and helps to protect it from unwelcome visitors.

LEFT: Little Barrier Island (Hauturu) was declared a wildlife sanctuary over a century ago.

BELOW RIGHT: The spectacular boulder beach on the south-west side of Little Barrier Island.

BELOW: Predators eliminated stitchbirds from the mainland, and they survived only on Little Barrier Island. However, they have since been transferred to other predator-free islands.

Early Maori occupation resulted in some forest on the western side of Little Barrier being logged for timber, but as the island has been declared a sanctuary for over 100 years, the forest has regenerated. With no deer or possums being introduced, the island remains in a relatively pristine state. But domestic cats had become feral and preyed on the abundant birdlife, especially the ground-nesting petrels. The rare endemic stitchbird, New Zealand's smallest honeyeater, found only on this island, was also severely threatened. However, after a difficult and sustained effort by the Wildlife Service, by 1978 cats were completely eradicated and stitchbird numbers increased so remarkably that transfers of the birds to other islands were initiated.

Another valuable island sanctuary is Kapiti Island in the north-western Cook Strait, off the west coast from Waikanae, north of Wellington. The possums and rats that once caused considerable damage have been eliminated, allowing several species of endangered birds to be introduced. For some years Kapiti Island was of importance in being the only remaining stronghold of the little spotted kiwi, a species that had become extinct on the mainland. Had it not been for the transfer to Kapiti of a few birds in 1912, the species would now be extinct. Several little spotted kiwi have now been transferred to other predator-free islands.

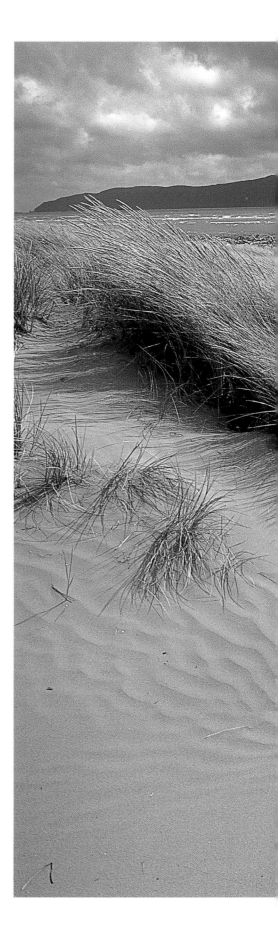

ABOVE: The little spotted kiwi is the smallest and rarest of the kiwis.

RIGHT: The Kapiti Island sanctuary (seen here offshore) is home to more than a thousand little spotted kiwi, as well as other endangered bird species.

ABOVE LEFT: A black robin. These birds are a conservation success story.

ABOVE: South East Island in the Chathams, together with Mangere Island, are the habitats of the black robin. This bird was miraculously saved from certain extinction: its poulation once included only one breeding female.

Tiritiri Matangi, in the Hauraki Gulf, is now a valuable predator-free open sanctuary. Many years ago the island was clothed in coastal mixed forest, but much of this was cleared by Maori settlers to provide areas for cultivation and dwellings. Later, European settlers continued to destroy forest to form pastures for sheep, cattle and goats, leaving only pockets of forest in the steep valleys. But in 1980 the island was declared a sanctuary. Volunteers and professional conservationists began a long process of replanting a forest with seedlings grown on the island. Today, with a thriving forest and removal of all mammalian predators, the island is a sanctuary for many species of endangered birds. As the island is an 'open' one and close to Auckland, visitors can experience the new growing forest, with the piping calls and intermingling of birdsong, which is rare in many mainland forests.

Many species of birds have evolved in isolation on some offshore and outlying islands to become subspecies with characteristics different from the mainland birds. The Chatham Island black robin is an example, and the fight to save this bird from extinction is well documented. Reduced to a population of only five birds in 1979, its numbers have been dramatically increased by a careful process of cross fostering. This was

ABOVE RIGHT: Sixty-two kakapo were known to survive in late 2000. Most of these now live on Codfish Island.

achieved by a robin's first clutch of eggs being placed in the nest of a Chatham Island tomtit, which incubated and fostered the chicks. In this way the robins were induced to lay a second clutch which they themselves reared.

Black robin numbers increased over several seasons and now occupy two small islands, Mangere Island and South East Island, close to the coast of Pitt Island in the Chathams. South East Island is also home to other rare birds and plants, notably the Chatham Island snipe, and the New Zealand shore plover. The New Zealand shore plover was once common around mainland coasts.

There are other ecologically valuable small islands close to Stewart Island. One of these is the forest-covered Whenua Hou or Codfish Island off the north-west coast. Possums and kiore have been exterminated and the island has now become the refuge of the highly endangered kakapo, the world's largest parrot.

Predator-free offshore islands are the safety net for New Zealand's endangered bird species. Just one accidental introduction of the smallest predator could be devastating. While the importance of these offshore islands is generally appreciated, their vulnerability is often forgotten.

THE COAST

…Sweet with salt
The free air wanders o'er the wandering waves…

– B.E. BAUGHAN

HABITATS OF THE COAST

New Zealand's coastline is one of the longest in the world relative to the country's landmass, with no part of the land being further than 130 kilometres from the sea. The topography varies considerably, with long surf-washed beaches spanning much of the west coast, interrupted by rocky headlands and cliffs. The east coast is more indented, with rocky outcrops and small islets sheltering bays of sandy or shingle beaches. Many of the larger sand beaches, particularly in the north, are backed by sand dunes.

In the South Island a distinct type of coastline exists. A complex of islands and drowned valleys form the maze-like Marlborough Sounds in the north and, in the south, Fiordland's spectacular, steep-sided sounds were carved out by glaciation during the last ice age.

The early Polynesian and European settlers destroyed the forests that originally grew on the east coasts of both the North and South Islands, although a remnant forest survives along the Catlins coast of Southland. Fiordland and parts of the west coast of the South Island, however, retain their virgin forests. Small areas of mixed forest, much of it second growth, still exist on some North Island coasts, with pohutukawa, karaka and puriri trees and nikau palms predominating. In parts of the South Island the southern rata may be seen in areas that have escaped browsing by possums. It is not generally realised what severe damage possums cause to rata and pohutukawa trees, killing them by defoliation. In some coastal regions, farm pastures now extend to the water's edge and cattle stray on to the beaches, browsing the shoreline vegetation; on occasions they can even be seen eating sea kelp. These locations are now devoid of trees except for a few pohutukawa, ngaio and other species.

Boulder beaches are a feature on some coasts, and where wave action is moderate, boulders retain their shape. However, on exposed shores boulders and pebbles constantly move against each other with the surge of breaking waves, and are an unsuitable habitat for marine life. On sheltered beaches the large rocks remain stable, forming a safe environment for marine life and therefore a valuable feeding ground for seabirds.

PREVIOUS PAGES: Te Arai beach on the east coast of Northland is a favourite habitat for several species of shorebirds, including a breeding population of the rare New Zealand fairy tern.

RIGHT: The extensive sand dunes of Parengarenga in Northland are a remote feeding and nesting haunt for many species of coastal birds.

BIRDLIFE OF THE COAST

Most coastal landscapes support a wide variety of birdlife, although shingle beaches are usually biologically unproductive. The sandy beaches provide a permanently moist environment for crustaceans, molluscs and marine worms, which in turn provide food for birds. Another rich source of food for birds are the sandhoppers and flies which inhabit the seaweed and flotsam washed up along the high-tide areas. The dunes backing some of these sandy beaches are favourite nesting sites for many species of shore birds such as terns, variable oystercatchers, dotterels and stilts.

However, in many areas marram grass and lupins have been planted to stabilise the dunes. The rampant growth of these plants has resulted in the gentle dune slopes being transformed into low, and in some cases, almost vertical, sand cliffs, with the marram grass, which blankets the landward dunes, creating a habitat unsuitable for nesting birds. The golden-coloured native pingao grass, which spreads out its long rhizomes to maintain a gentle sloping of the sand dunes, and provide a favourable habitat for nesting dotterels and oystercatchers, has now frequently been replaced by marram grass.

Rocky shores generally support rich beds of seaweed or bull kelp. Shags and penguins often swim and fish among the deep, sea-moving kelp and, at low tide, gulls feed on the varieties of marine organisms they find hidden in the kelp. Above the high-water mark these shores also sustain growths of succulent ice-plants and grasses, often being backed by vegetation which will withstand salt-laden winds. These include coastal flax, ngaio, wind-tolerant taupata and pohutukawa trees, their tough roots helping to stabilise sea cliffs.

The flowers of some coastal vegetation provide nectar. The upright branches of flax plants produce russet, nectar-bearing flowers, with the massed red blooms of the pohutukawa tree also producing nectar. The salt-laden winds constantly shape much of the coastal vegetation, limiting growth, especially along exposed west coast beaches. In order to survive, some vegetation has evolved into a prostrate form, with longer branches growing towards the favourable side, away from the wind, and the branches which face the onslaught of the wind become stunted or curled sideways. The open surf beaches often lack birdlife, except for the large black-backed gull and the smaller red-billed gulls.

Several species of birds inhabit the rocky Kaikoura Peninsula. In particular, New Zealand's largest colony of nesting red-billed gulls is established here, together with nesting white-fronted terns. Other species, such as herons, turnstones and, occasionally, wandering tattler, feed on marine organisms, found along the large rock platform.

LEFT: Endemic white-fronted terns are widespread around mainland coastlines.

LEFT: A typical surf beach in Westland. Surf beaches do not usually provide food for many birds.

BELOW: The red-billed gull is common around the coasts. It also occurs inland at Lake Rotorua, where it nests in colonies with the endemic black-billed gull. Very occasionally these birds hybridise.

Gulls

All gulls are scavengers, unlike the terns that feed only on live fish captured by making shallow dives offshore. The black-backed gull survives in many habitats and is a well-known scavenger, feeding on carrion washed ashore and storm-wrecked birds. But the gull also takes insects, molluscs and shellfish, with the shellfish often being carried high in the air, then dropped, so that the shell breaks on rocks below. Most pairs of black-backed gulls nest in loose colonies near the seashore, in rough nests composed of grasses and seaweed, and others nest in isolation or on rocky headlands, while others may nest inland.

LEFT: The tough roots of pohutukawa trees help to stabilise sea cliffs.

BELOW: A black-backed gull at its nest near a shingle beach. Some pairs nest in isolation inland or on rocky headlands. Others nest in loose colonies.

ABOVE: The Australasian gannet's wingspan reaches two metres.

LEFT: A mainland gannet colony at Muriwai on the Auckland west coast.

Gannets

The majestic gannet, with its near 2-metre wingspan, usually dives for fish in the open sea, but sometimes cruises close to breakers, feeding in the shallow water. Gannets nest in large colonies on selected offshore islands and stacks. Until comparatively recently, the only colony nesting on the mainland was one at Cape Kidnappers in Hawke's Bay. But a few years ago, due to overcrowding of the colony on Oaia Island off Auckland's west coast at Muriwai, birds commenced nesting on a small stack close to the mainland cliffs. More recently gannets have chosen to nest on the adjacent mainland, where they are protected by a fence erected by the Auckland Regional Council. Another small colony also nests on Farewell Spit.

Variable oystercatchers, dotterels and terns

Sandy beaches and dunes, particularly on the east coasts, are favourite nesting habitats for other shore birds such as variable oystercatchers, dotterels and terns. The endemic variable oystercatcher, as its name implies, is the only oystercatcher in the world which displays dimorphic, or variable, plumage, with some being pied, others showing small patches of white feathers, while some, especially on Stewart Island, are completely black. The birds are frequently seen in pairs, although they tend to flock in winter months.

ABOVE: Sheltered harbours and estuaries provide rich sources of food for several shore and wading bird species such as these oystercatchers seen here feeding in the shallows.

ABOVE: Native pingao grass, which helps to stabilise the sand dunes, also provides shelter and concealment for a variable oystercatcher and its newly hatched chick.

ABOVE: Unlike most terns, the rare New Zealand fairy tern nests in isolation, on a few remote sandy beaches on the east coast of Northland.

RIGHT: A pair of Caspian terns with their chicks. Chicks are sometimes fed fish too large to swallow, as in the case of this sand-covered flounder.

The Caspian tern, a cosmopolitan species and the largest of the terns, nests in colonies among the dunes of favoured beach sites. Like other terns, they use no nesting material. The clutch of two or three eggs is laid in a scrape in the sand, and due to the effects of the wind the scrape may fill in, but is frequently reformed by the sitting bird rotating and kicking out the encroaching sand.

The common white-fronted tern, or kahawai bird, also nests in colonies, sometimes congregating on sand dunes, but more often choosing such sites as rocky islets close to the shore, or shellbanks.

In contrast, the rare fairy tern, the smallest of the terns, being no larger than a blackbird, nests in isolation on a few east coast beaches of north Auckland. It is probable that approximately 10 pairs now nest in New Zealand, and the Department of Conservation has formulated a recovery plan for this species. The nest of this tiny tern is usually sited on the sand among broken seashells, and is sometimes placed too close to the sea, leaving it vulnerable to being washed away during storms.

The endemic New Zealand dotterel is a threatened species, and is the subject of a recovery plan. Unusually distributed, it occurs north of the eastern Bay of Plenty and Raglan, as well as on Stewart Island. The Stewart Island dotterel is now classed as a distinct subspecies. The northern subspecies nests on sand dunes near driftwood or pingao grass, the rim of the sandy nest-scrape often decorated with shells. The Stewart Island subspecies nests above the bushline on rocky high country ground.

Shags and cormorants

Many species of shags or cormorants live around the coasts. Some strikingly beautiful species live only on inaccessible offshore islands, but the attractive spotted shag is easily seen around rocky coasts, when, after the breeding season, birds congregate on rocks close to the shore to rest between spells of fishing.

The favourite nesting sites for spotted shags are on ledges of cliff faces near deep water, and in alcoves and fissures in volcanic cliffs, such as those on Banks Peninsula and Auckland's west coast. But the large coast-dwelling pied shag prefers more sheltered shores than does the spotted shag. The pied shag nests in trees overhanging cliffs, with pohutukawa being a species commonly used for this purpose. The host trees eventually die, as the bird has a habit of defoliating the tree and scorching the leaves with caustic excrement.

Shags regularly dry their plumage by perching on a rock or branch with wings outstretched, as their feathers are not fully waterproofed. This lack of waterproofing has the advantage of rendering the body less buoyant, so that less energy is expended when swimming submerged in search of fish.

LEFT TOP: The New Zealand dotterel usually nests on sandy and shell beaches where its nests are subject to predation by mustelids, feral cats and black-billed gulls. Many nests are destroyed by high tides coinciding with storms.

LEFT BOTTOM: Newly hatched New Zealand dotterel chicks.

BELOW: Spotted shags are a marine species and often fish far out at sea. They nest on rocky cliff ledges.

Penguins

The blue penguin, the smallest penguin in the world, is sometimes seen swimming close to the coast. It comes ashore at night to roost or nest in caves, rock crevices or in burrows beneath tree roots. The rare yellow-eyed penguin is a much larger bird. Its distribution is restricted to the east coast of the South Island, south from Otago and on islands around Stewart Island. This species comes ashore during daylight hours when it visits its nest in coastal scrub or flax. The Fiordland crested penguin occurs on the south-west coasts of the South Island as well as on islands around Stewart Island. All penguins moult, a process that takes up to three weeks. During this time the birds remain ashore in seclusion, and do not feed. Prior to this fasting, penguins fatten up by feeding heavily at sea. The old plumage is pushed out by the new blue sheathed feathers, with the penguin at first looking prickly like a hedgehog.

Reef herons

The reef heron is a wary bird, slightly smaller and stockier than the familiar white-faced heron. It is decreasing in numbers on the coasts, due to disturbance by recreational boats. The heron prefers to live on rocky shores where it feeds along the tide line or in rock pools. As the bird feeds in shallow water, it assumes a typical low, semi-crouching attitude, with wings spread umbrella-like over the water, to prevent reflection from the sky. The substantial nest of sticks is built by the reef heron in isolated, inaccessible caves or rock fissures and sometimes beneath exposed pohutukawa roots.

Although much of the New Zealand coastline has been modified in various ways, it is still possible to visit many secluded beaches, wild rocky shores and coastal birdlife haunts within a short distance of most of the country's towns and cities.

RIGHT: Blue penguins come ashore to roost only after dark.

BELOW: A yellow-eyed penguin emerges from the surf to visit its nest.

HARBOURS AND ESTUARIES

...White glittering squadrons on the level mud
Dressing their lines before the enclosing flood...

– A. DOMETT

HABITATS OF HARBOURS AND ESTUARIES

At first glance the wide, muddy expanses of New Zealand's harbours and estuaries at low tide present an uninviting and desolate landscape. Yet this is a habitat rich with marine life.

A transformation occurs in these tidal regions approximately every 12 hours. At high tide the sea fills the estuary with a broad sheet of calm, glistening water right up to the fringes of the mangrove and salt marsh. Then, as the sea slowly recedes, an expanse of mud or sand is revealed, laced with a network of narrow channels and rivulets.

Mangrove trees grow in most sheltered harbours and estuaries of the northern regions and apart from providing feeding areas for waders, research has shown them to be valuable breeding grounds for many species of fish. Mangrove trees, which grow in thick mud and are starved of oxygen, have 'breathing roots' (pneumatophores) which stand several centimetres above the mud. These trees are often associated with salt marshes that support certain low-growing varieties of succulents, sedges and rushes and are sometimes backed by flax, rushes and raupo on the landward side. During high spring tides salt marshes are inundated, with many of the lower branches of mangroves being immersed in the sea. Mangroves, salicornia and sedges have evolved to withstand the flooding of sea water with each high tide.

PREVIOUS PAGES: Late sunlight spotlights a flight of wrybills.

BELOW: High tides inundate the salt marsh sedges and mangroves.

RIGHT: The rising tide at dawn floods the emerging young mangroves.

In the past, the salt marshes and tracts of mangrove were seen as convenient locations to establish dumps for the disposal of town refuse, or reclamation sites for land-hungry developers. However, there has been a growing appreciation of the importance of these natural environments. In 1973 the Auckland City Council proposed to use the Glen Innes spit area in the Tamaki Estuary as the site for a rubbish dump. A vigorous campaign by local residents and conservationists, led by naturalist and writer, the late Ronald Lockley, resulted in the area being saved for posterity. The spit is now a valuable natural reserve frequented by several species of shore birds.

BIRDLIFE OF HARBOURS AND ESTUARIES

In the early morning, as the dawn sky lightens and reflects in the still water creeping across the mudflats, small groups of birds in turn take wing as their feeding is interrupted by the incoming tide. There is a certain excitement in the air, with skeins of godwits and knots hurtling along just above the surface of the water, their wings rustling in the calm air as they seek a place to rest.

LEFT: Coastal sedges are a favourite nesting site for the shy banded rail. The surrounding stems of sedges are bent overhead, providing a bower to protect the nest from the overhead hunt of harriers.

BELOW: Four eastern curlews, the largest of the migrant waders, fly away with bar-tailed godwits and oystercatchers.

ABOVE: An immature New Zealand kingfisher with a mud crab. Kingfishers are found on sheltered coasts, in wetlands, open country and even in the depths of forests.

RIGHT: A fernbird brings a feather to its nest among coastal sedges. Fernbirds usually keep to low, dense vegetation.

Always, with the rising tide, birds are driven from the mudflats. As waders seek favourite roosting sites, they rise in glimmering, swerving clouds, their flurry of wings whipping the air with a rush of wind, before they settle again on the sand and shell banks. In some harbours roosting space is restricted and this is a restless time for waders as they wait for the falling tide. They shuffle together on the banks, often taking impatient flights to seek other shell banks, then returning and, with a flash of dipping wings, suddenly drop to the shore.

Several species of small birds, such as silvereyes, feed on insects in the foliage of mangroves, and kingfishers may often be seen on a prominent perch waiting to dive for small fish or mud crabs. Although fairly common in some estuaries and harbours, the secretive banded rail is seldom seen. This handsome little bantam-like bird may be glimpsed as it runs rapidly beneath the mangroves, or perches in a mangrove branch at high tide.

The sedges and rushes of the salt marsh provide good nesting and feeding sites for fernbirds, banded rails and occasionally bitterns. Fernbirds usually build a nest close to the base of a clump of sedge and nests may be flooded by high spring tides when the birds have not made allowance for the rising water. Fernbirds' nests are also subject to predation by rats, which sometimes forage in these sites.

ABOVE: Three red-necked stints with a sharp-tailed sandpiper. The sparrow-sized red-necked stint is the smallest migrant wader to visit New Zealand shores.

At low tide, with the mudflats and sand exposed, the estuaries provide extensive and abundant feeding grounds for a wide range of bird species. In winter months most of these are the resident ducks, shags, herons, gulls, terns, dotterels, wrybills, oystercatchers and pied stilts, while occasionally Caspian terns fly overhead, searching for fish.

Migrant waders

In summer months, migrant waders are the most obvious birdlife scattered across the open estuarine mudflats and flocked along shelly shorelines. The annual visitation of these migrant wading birds makes a dramatic display. They range in size from the long-billed curlew with its 18-centimetre-long curved bill, to the tiny red-necked stint, only fractionally larger than a house-sparrow. Huge flocks of these migrants reach New Zealand shores in late September or early October, having completed a journey of thousands of kilometres from the tundra regions of Siberia, where they have fed and nested during the brief arctic summer.

By far the best known and most numerous of these migrants is the bar-tailed godwit, with over 100,000 arriving each summer in New Zealand. They are usually seen probing for marine organisms in the mud, or resting in flocks on shell banks and sandspits at high tide. Godwits, and to a lesser extent the smaller knots, far outnumber other species of migrant waders which arrive in New Zealand estuaries, such as turnstones and several species of sandpipers.

It is amazing that tiny birds, such as the diminutive stint, have the ability to navigate thousands of kilometres, much of this distance over ocean, to spend the summer months feeding in some of New Zealand's harbours. Most of these migrants arrive from late September, lean and anxious to feed, their plumage a drab grey or brown. However, by February or March the birds have moulted, put on weight and assumed a colourful nuptial plumage. Most males are more obviously brightly coloured than the females. They are ready then to make the return journey north to nest in the tundra. The dramatic russet colouring assumed by the waders before they leave New Zealand blends with the similarly coloured low tundra vegetation of the Siberian nesting grounds. This offers the birds and their shallow nests some camouflage protection from predation by foxes and hawks.

As the waders spread out across the bare mudflats to feed over the summer months, the birds often intermingle, but there is a behavioural relationship between them which separates their feeding patterns. The birds find crustaceans and marine worms, with the godwits using their long bills to probe deeply into the mud and others, with their shorter bills, feeding closer to the surface. The longer legs of the godwits also allows them to feed along the edges of deeper water. Various birds employ different motions with their bills to feed, such as the 'sideways scooping' movement of terek sandpipers. Turnstones, as their name suggests, snatch organisms by turning over small stones and shells. And the tiny stint, feeding on invertebrates, rapidly triggers its bill across the wet mud like a sewing machine. With these diverse feeding habits, the different species tend not to compete with each other for food.

Above: The terek sandpiper is recognised by its upturned bill.

Below: Bar-tailed godwits are the most numerous of the migrant waders to visit New Zealand's shores.

Indigenous waders

Many indigenous wading birds use the tidal habitats as feeding grounds throughout the year. Of these, the conspicuous South Island pied oystercatchers are by far the most numerous, with fewer numbers of pied stilts, banded dotterels and the unique endemic wrybill plovers. All these species are migratory within New Zealand, although some banded dotterels also fly to eastern Australia and Tasmania to spend the winter. Even though the South Island pied oystercatchers occur in their thousands in North Island locations, they nest only in the South Island, choosing shingle riverbeds, pastures or ploughed land on which to lay their eggs in a scrape in the ground.

BELOW: A flight of South Island pied oystercatchers.

Wrybills are also seen throughout the year on many North Island estuaries and mudflats, but in early spring mature birds migrate to the South Island to nest on the shingle fans of certain rivers. These small plovers, which are found only in New Zealand, are unique in that their bill tips twist to the right, an adaptation which is thought to facilitate the capture of invertebrates when probing for food under river stones.

All waders are gregarious, active birds, feeding in loose flocks. As each tide rises they are driven from their feeding grounds to roost in large congregations on exposed shell banks and sandspits. It is not uncommon to see flocks of several thousand birds massed on high-tide roosts in locations such as Parengarenga, Kaipara and Manukau Harbours, Miranda in the Firth of Thames, Farewell Spit, the Heathcote Estuary in Christchurch, Lake Ellesmere and other estuaries further south.

The most spectacular sight of massed waders occurs when resident and migrant waders are assembled in mixed flocks. The greatest concentration of mixed flocks occurs from February to April, when resident waders take up their places in the estuaries after nesting and the migrants are just preparing for the flight to the northern hemisphere.

ABOVE: The endemic wrybill is unique in that the tip of its bill twists to the right. Wrybills nest only in the South Island, but migrate to North Island harbours and estuaries after the nesting season.

RIGHT: As the high tide begins to ebb and expose their mudflat feeding grounds, flocks of restless wrybills take wing before finding another sandspit roost.

Herons

White-faced herons are common in most of these habitats. Large numbers of this Australian bird arrived in New Zealand about 50 years ago. They rapidly colonised marine and freshwater wetlands in both the North and South Islands. They employ a variety of methods to feed. Sometimes they stand motionless, waiting for a fish to come within reach of a lightning jab from their rapier-like bill; at other times they move stealthily along the edge of the tide, searching for prey. When feeding in shallow pools, they rake the mud, with one foot extended, to disturb marine organisms.

During winter months the white heron, or kotuku, may be seen in coastal and swampy lagoon and estuarine areas in a few North Island habitats, but is more frequently located throughout the South Island. The only breeding site for this bird is in the trees bordering the Waitangiroto Stream in south Westland. A noticeable feature of the breeding white heron is the changed colour of its bill, from the normal yellow to black. Following the summer nesting season, these strikingly large white birds disperse throughout the country.

LEFT: White-faced herons are by far the commonest of the five species of heron to be found in New Zealand.

BELOW: A white heron or kotuku. This cosmopolitan species nest in a colony in south Westland.

Royal spoonbills

Another conspicuous white bird, slightly smaller than the white heron, is the royal spoonbill. For many years these birds nested in tall trees close to the white heron colony in south Westland. Since 1978 several pairs have nested on the ground in the salt marshes of the Vernon Lagoons in Marlborough. Unfortunately, some nests have been washed over on occasions when high spring tides have coincided with floodwaters from the adjacent Wairau River. However, spoonbills have increased in number during recent years, having successfully nested in Northland and on an island off the Otago coast. Spoonbills feed in their own particular way. Often in groups, they wade along in shallow water, swinging their spatulate bills from side to side to sieve out marine organisms.

The familiar landscapes of harbour and estuary are common throughout New Zealand, and some of the most ecologically important of them lie close to towns and cities. Within comparatively small areas these environments provide a constantly changing scene, activated by the movement of the tides and the needs of dependent wildlife.

RIGHT: A pair of royal spoonbills at their nest. Some pairs also nest in trees adjacent to the white heron colony.

BELOW: Unlike herons, spoonbills fly with their necks extended.

COUNTRYSIDE

...Grass springs sweet where once thick forest
gripped vales by fire and axe freed to pasturage...

– U. Bethell

HABITATS OF THE COUNTRYSIDE

Of all this country's changed environments, the development of the present rural landscape from the original forest has undoubtedly been the most dramatic. Today, farmed grasslands and arable cultivation occupy more than half the New Zealand landmass.

The early European settlers found many regions already denuded of the original forest. Much of this was scrub-covered and easily cleared and burned, so introduced species of grasses and clover readily germinated and grew in the ashes. In other areas, more forest was cleared for pasture establishment as well as to provide timber for building. Deforestation rapidly gained momentum, to include steep hill country. The consequence of this was the erosion of soil and flooding of lowland regions, a phenomenon which frequently still occurs.

The cultivation of arable farming was mainly confined to the South Island and extensive grain-growing crops were developed, particularly on the

PREVIOUS PAGES: Patterns of pasture and arable land in Hawke's Bay.

BELOW: King Country hill country pastures. Introduced exotic deciduous trees provide shade for cattle and sheep in summer, then permit the warmth of sunlight through in winter.

plains of Canterbury, Otago and parts of Southland. Differing regional climates and soil types have today created a variety of pasture associations. With the combination of the use of fertilisers and a favourable climate, New Zealand has some of the most productive pastures in the world.

However, this has been to the detriment of the country's native trees, which have almost vanished from the farm landscape. Instead rows of exotics such as macrocarpa trees provide windbreaks and in some places pine plantations are relieved with plantings of exotic deciduous trees. Yellow broom and gorse were introduced to form hedgerows but have spread uncontrolled in some regions.

Orchards and vineyards have been established for many years in climatically suitable regions of both the North and South Islands. This diversification of cultivation provides suitable habitats for many birds. European species were introduced by early settlers for nostalgic reasons, and most of these birds have thrived in their new environment.

BELOW: Dairy cattle grazing a Waikato pasture. The Waikato and Taranaki regions of the North Island are noted for the high production of their pastureland.

ABOVE: Yellowhammers and other finch species were introduced from Britain in the 1860s for nostalgic reasons. They are a common sight in the countryside.

RIGHT: Goldfinches, introduced from Britain, are now more numerous in New Zealand than in their country of origin. In winter they congregate in very large flocks, feeding on seeds from grasses and thistles. '

BIRDLIFE OF THE COUNTRYSIDE

Blackbirds, starlings and chaffinches may be familiar to many New Zealanders in their gardens and parks, but they have also become a common sight in the open country. The attractive 'charms' of goldfinches have fared so well in New Zealand that they are considered to be more numerous here than in England, their land of origin. In winter, when they congregate to feed on seeds and thistle heads, swarms of over 1000 birds are not uncommon. Goldfinches build dainty nests composed of fine grasses, lichens, moss and cobwebs woven into a neat cup. Favourite sites are in the branches of apple, plum and other orchard trees.

Starlings are useful to the farmer as they often scatter in flocks across pastureland to feed on grass grubs. Black-billed gulls may sometimes unite with the starlings as they follow the farmer's plough, enjoying a feast of disturbed grubs. Starlings frequent different habitats, and benefit from nest boxes built for them in the country, as well as in urban areas. In the evening starlings usually congregate in large trees to roost.

ABOVE: A skylark with its chicks. The introduced skylark is sometimes confused with the similarly coloured pipit. But most skylarks prefer to feed in short pastures and cultivated land, whereas the pipit is found on the coast, in rough pastures and in the high country.

There would be a dearth of birdsong in the open country but for the presence of the skylark, another European settler. As it soars into the sky the trilling, warbling song of the skylark spills without pause through the air. Skylarks build a well-concealed nest in a depression in the ground, usually beneath a clump of grass but often in very short, grazed pasture. When sitting on its nest, the bird is very well camouflaged but, in spite of this, eggs and chicks are often taken by the introduced Australian white-backed magpie and by hedgehogs.

The Indian myna, first introduced to Canterbury, has gradually deserted the south for the warmer temperatures of northern New Zealand. They are a common sight on roadsides where they scavenge insects killed by traffic and are noted for their uncanny ability to dodge vehicles. Unfortunately, mynas have a detrimental effect on several of New Zealand's smaller native birds, taking eggs or chicks from nests, particularly the grey warbler. They have also been known to eject kingfishers from their nest holes.

Harriers are a common sight as they quarter the land and roadsides hunting insects, small birds and carrion. And sometimes it is possible to glimpse Californian quail with their tiny bumblebee-like chicks tripping along the roadside before disappearing into the safety of wild grasses.

ABOVE: A harrier nest in a hayfield. It is more usual for harriers to nest in beds of raupo or the sedges of swampland.

RIGHT: A pastoral scene bordering native forest.

Native species

While pastures, arable land and orchards provide favourable living conditions for most of the introduced birds, some of New Zealand's native species have also found these open habitats to their liking. The pukeko favours the wetter paddocks and are often seen on the grass verges of busy motorways. In the South Island pastures and ploughed land are favourite feeding and nesting grounds for the conspicuous South Island pied oystercatcher. Here it is frequently joined by black-fronted terns and black-billed gulls searching for insects. Paradise shelducks are increasing in numbers and may be seen in pastoral open country.

The keen, bright-feathered kingfisher often perches on powerlines or tall posts in open pastureland. Here it is in a good position to dive suddenly on insects, lizards or earthworms. The 'catch' is taken back to the perch where larger prey is repeatedly bashed, until it is limp enough to be swallowed whole, and head first.

Australian arrivals

From time to time, aided by the prevailing westerly winds, Australian birds cross the Tasman, and in this way are self-introduced to New Zealand. Previously many of these bird species, accustomed to living in open country, would not have found the original forest habitat suitable and could not have survived. However, the expanded rural landscape here has proved agreeable for a number of these birds.

BELOW: Pukeko are frequently seen feeding on pastureland, but are more common in wetlands.

BOTTOM: The endemic paradise shelduck inhabit pastures, wetlands and high country.

RIGHT: New Zealand kingfishers possess acute eyesight. From high perches they swoop on their catch.

A good example is the Australian spur-winged plover. Birds were first noted in Southland in 1932, where they settled and bred. Numbers increased steadily over the years and birds invaded other suitable areas. They eventually spread to the North Island in the early 1970s and today the bird is a noticeable inhabitant of open country throughout both main islands. Spur-winged plovers make a distinctive rattling call and fly in a typical floppy, lapwing fashion. Out of the breeding season they often congregate in large flocks in estuaries and wetlands.

Other Australian birds which have recently settled in New Zealand open country are the white-faced heron and the welcome swallow. Both species arrived in large numbers in the 1950s and spread rapidly. Besides feeding in open, wet pastures, the white-faced heron now occupies a variety of habitats and is quite at home in a marine environment or on the borders of inland freshwater lakes. These herons usually nest high in pine trees, where they are sometimes harassed by magpies who may be nesting nearby. The magpie builds a substantial nest of sticks, grasses and leaves, often lining this with wool gleaned from fences where sheep have rubbed. These nests may be built in trees such as pohutukawa or more frequently in pines and macrocarpa.

LEFT: White-faced herons usually choose tall pine trees in which to build their nest composed of sticks.

BELOW: Spur-winged plovers, self-introduced from Australia to Southland in 1932, bred successfully and are now common in farmland, wetlands and sheltered estuaries and harbours. They are suspected of predating nests of ground nesting birds.

In recent years, large flocks of cattle egrets have been arriving in New Zealand each autumn, presumably from Australia. They spend the winter and spring keeping company with cattle and feeding on the grubs and insects which these animals disturb. These cattle egrets are cosmopolitan, being the same species of egret which feeds with animals in Africa, sometimes hitching rides on the backs of elephants. In late October, having assumed breeding plumage, the egrets fly back to nest in Australia. It is hoped that these attractive small herons will one day remain to nest in New Zealand.

As this open farmland has now proved valuable to a wide variety of birds, it has also resulted in the disappearance of others. These are usually forest birds which need the protection and food that only a forest can offer, and many have not survived the clearance of their habitat. Others have escaped and found adequate shelter in remote verges of forest, while some birds have adapted to live successfully in the rural landscape.

RIGHT TOP: Cattle egrets migrate here from Australia each autumn, returning there to nest in early summer. The birds feed on insects and earthworms, disturbed by the feet of cattle.

RIGHT BOTTOM: The welcome swallow is another self-introduced Australian settler and is found throughout the country. They feed on insects caught on the wing and their nests, formed of grasses combined with mud, are built under bridges or farm outhouses.

BELOW: White-backed and black-backed magpies were introduced from Australia and inhabit pastureland throughout New Zealand. They often predate the eggs and chicks of ground nesting birds.

WETLANDS

...O let them be left, wildness and wet;
Long live the weeds and the wilderness yet...

– GERARD MANLEY HOPKINS

HABITATS OF WETLANDS

New Zealand's wetland habitats are well distributed throughout the country, encompassing lakes, rivers, swamps, bogs and lagoons. They nourish a wide diversity of birdlife.

Lakes

The lakes were formed in different ways. The largest, Lake Taupo and those of the central plateau in the Rotorua district, are of volcanic origin. Others have been formed by earthquakes which uplifted the land, blocking drainage from low-lying areas or, as in the case of Lake Waikaremoana, where a massive earthquake-induced landslide blocked the exit of a river valley. This occurred only 2200 years ago, a fact confirmed by carbon-dating of dead trees in the drowned valley.

Many of the South Island lakes were carved out by glacial action during the last ice age, and a number of these are very deep. Some are a turquoise colour with a milky appearance due to their content of 'rock flour', ground from alpine rocks by glacial action.

By preventing drainage, wind-blown sand has created dune lakes in many coastal areas. In other cases, such as Lake Ellesmere, the sea's wave action has built up a long shingle bar to isolate the lake from the sea.

Constructed lakes are also a feature of the New Zealand landscape. Most of these are long and narrow, having been formed by damming river systems to provide water storage for generating electricity. Lake Benmore, fed by rivers of the Waitaki catchment, is the largest of these hydro-storage lakes, covering nearly 80 square kilometres. Many of these lakes have been attractively landscaped with trees and areas set aside for picnicking, boating and fishing. Smaller artificial lakes are used as water-supply reservoirs for town and city use. Access to most of these lakes is restricted, and many have been formed in fairly remote areas.

PREVIOUS PAGES: Lake McGregor, a high country lake in South Canterbury, is a habitat for many waterbirds, including the Australasian crested grebe.

ABOVE: In winter months paradise shelduck congregate on freshwater lagoons.

RIGHT: The Rakaia River, one of the South Island's braided rivers.

LEFT: An Australasian bittern at its nest in a raupo swamp. This extremely shy bird is related to the herons. The female bittern performs the incubation of the eggs and feeding of the chicks.

BELOW: Lake Whakamaru, formed by one of the Waikato River hydro-electric dams, is an excellent habitat for many species of waterfowl, including crakes and bittern.

Fluctuating water levels in hydro-storage lakes and reservoirs affects the aesthetic appearance of all these lakes and may have an effect on their ecology, by eroding shorelines or drying out banks so that vegetation dies. The hydro lakes, particularly the newer ones, are often very deep and so do not support the water organisms or weeds that would attract birdlife. Wave action occurs on the large lakes, and raupo and rushes tend to grow only where they are protected from this disruption. But lakes which are shallow-rimmed and edged with clumps of rushes and water vegetation prove favourable habitats for ducks, shags, herons, stilts and other waterbirds.

Lake Whakamaru, the fourth hydro lake created on the Waikato River, is bordered by stretches of rushes and shallow, weed-fringed water. This attracts many species of wetland birds; even the shy bittern feeds and nests here.

Some of the South Island artificial lakes support populations of ducks, paradise shelducks and Canada geese. However, it is the natural lakes which generally attract the greatest numbers of wetland birds. Lake Ellesmere and Lake Wairarapa are particularly rich in birdlife, and the endemic New Zealand scaup, the country's only true diving duck, is found only in clearwater lakes. The duck obtains all its food by swimming efficiently below the surface of the water.

TOP: The scaup's diet is made up of the aquatic plants, snails and insects to be found at the bottom of clearwater lakes.

BOTTOM: The Australian coot was self-introduced to the South Island's Lake Hayes in 1958 where they bred successfully. They now inhabit many lakes throughout New Zealand.

RIGHT: Grey teal are increasing in number throughout New Zealand. They readily use artificial nest boxes provided in some wetland habitats.

The natural subalpine lakes of the South Island are the remaining strongholds of the Australasian crested grebe, a species once living on some North Island lakes. The highest population of this aquatic bird is found on Lake Alexandrina in South Canterbury. The crested grebe, being entirely aquatic, lives on a diet of fish and aquatic insects. It obtains all its food by diving, often remaining submerged for up to 50 seconds. As the crested grebe rears its chicks by feeding them with fish, the parent also occasionally adds small feathers with the food, presumably to prevent bones being caught in the chick's gut. A close relative is the New Zealand dabchick, a much smaller bird, which now seems absent from its former haunts in the South Island. However, it is still reasonably common on many North Island lakes, particularly those of the central plateau and the northern dune lakes.

TOP: A New Zealand dabchick brings food to its chick, which is carried on the other parent's back. The pair take turns to carry their chicks.

ABOVE: A pair of black swans with their cygnets. Black swans are very common in many wetland habitats, including saltwater inlets.

LEFT: An Australasian crested grebe on its nest composed of sticks and waterweed, on a South Island high country lake.

Rivers

The major rivers of the North Island radiate to the coasts from the central mountains and the volcanic plateau. New Zealand's longest river, the Waikato, nearly 450 kilometres in length, flows from its source on the eastern side of Mount Ruapehu into Lake Taupo via the Tongariro River. From the lake's outlet it reaches the Tasman Sea at the Waikato Heads.

Many South Island rivers are fast-flowing as they originate from high country or from the Southern Alps. Lakes are also the source of some rivers. The fast-flowing Buller River commences its course to the West Coast from Lake Rotoiti. Further south, the Waiau River flows from Lake Te Anau into Lake Manapouri and then to the Southland coast. Its volume has been adversely affected by the use of Lake Manapouri water to supply the power station which releases its water into Doubtful Sound.

Some of the most ecologically interesting rivers are the braided shingle rivers of Canterbury and the Waitaki River catchment, which all arise on

the eastern side of the Southern Alps. Braided rivers are those which interweave channels with shingle islands; the channels often changing course when there is a fluctuation in water flows. Internationally, braided rivers of the type found in New Zealand are uncommon, and the specialised avifauna which have evolved and adapted to live and breed in these habitats are found nowhere else in the world.

These rivers, which are subject to rapid fluctuations in level, provide more extensive habitats for the resident birds than single-channel rivers. Typical of the birds feeding and nesting on these rivers is the unique wrybill, previously mentioned, when it visits North Island feeding grounds out of the breeding season. The adult wrybill's cryptic colouring matches the stones of its river habitat and, unless the bird is moving, it is difficult to see. Chicks too are well camouflaged. Similarly, the eggs, laid in a hollow among the stones on shingle fans in the river, are the colour of the river stones.

LEFT TOP: Black-fronted terns feed and nest on South Island shingle rivers. They also feed on insects caught on agricultural land.

LEFT BELOW: The Whirinaki River flows through native forests in the northern Urewera National Park. It is one of the rivers inhabited by blue duck.

BELOW: Wrybills nest on shingle fans of a few South Island braided rivers.

Other endemic bird species found on these braided rivers are the black-fronted tern, the black-billed gull and the banded dotterel. Whereas the wrybill nests only on certain braided rivers, the black-billed gull and black-fronted tern also nest and feed on other South Island stony rivers. The black-fronted dotterel, an immigrant from Australia, lives and nests on the shingle rivers of Hawke's Bay, but has also spread to some rivers in the South Island.

The endemic black stilt, now the rarest wader in the world, uses the Waitaki River catchment as its only nesting habitat. Its survival is threatened by the presence of a high number of predatory mustelids and feral cats in the area. These predators were originally attracted to prey on the multitude of rabbits which run wild in this part of the country. Some of the black stilt's former habitats have been severely modified by the colossal schemes to harness water for power generation in the Waitaki

ABOVE: A banded dotterel incubating eggs at its nest on a shingle riverbed. The birds also nest in stony paddocks and on some sandy beaches.

RIGHT TOP: Black-fronted dotterels feed and nest on shingle riverbeds in Hawke's Bay. They have recently spread to some South Island areas.

RIGHT BOTTOM: The endemic black stilt is the world's rarest wading bird. They nest only in the South Island's Waitaki River catchment region. After nesting, some birds winter in the North Island.

River catchment. Wide canals now divert water from the Tekapo, Pukaki and Ohau rivers to power stations, and then supply water to Lake Benmore. Because of these changes, the rivers now have extremely low flow rates and are no longer attractive habitats for black stilts. Fortunately, the ecologically important Ahuriri River, apart from some use of water for farmland irrigation, has not been exploited for power generation. This is a favoured habitat for the black stilt.

Many South Island shingle riverbeds have been modified by infestation with exotic vegetation such as broom, lupins and willows. Some North Island rivers have been similarly affected, but not to the same extent. The plants bring colour and beauty to these wetlands, but they deny large expanses of shingle to river birds for their feeding and nesting. Willows in particular, with their low-sweeping branches and exposed roots, cause problems by restricting water flows.

Some well-known waterfalls are found on the major rivers and because of its proximity to the main highway, Huka Falls on the Waikato River is probably the best known of these. In fact many of the most impressive waterfalls are found on some of the smaller rivers and streams, especially in the high country, Fiordland and other high rainfall regions. However, in these regions, a number of waterfalls only function after periods of continuous heavy rain. Not all waterfalls are river-fed, as in the instance of the famous Sutherland Falls in Fiordland. These falls, which are the highest in New Zealand, are released from Lake Quill, a small alpine lake. Waterfalls and rapids are common on many high-country turbulent rivers, and these are habitats favoured by the endemic blue duck.

Swamps

The country's landscape originally included large expanses of swamp-land, some of it interspersed with swamp-forest trees, such as kahikatea. Much of the Waikato Basin and Hauraki Plains consisted of this type of vegetation. Today, few large areas of swamp and bog remain, most of it having been drained for agricultural use. A classic example of drainage occurred in 1864, when a huge portion of Canterbury swampland was drained to form the Longbeach Estate. Altogether, 250 kilometres of open drains were excavated to produce a highly productive farm.

The type of vegetation growing in swampland is dependent on the nutrient content of the soil and water. Where fertility is high, flax, raupo and carex sedges flourish, whereas in low-fertility regions the only tall plants may be the jointed and rush-like sedges. All unmodified swamps provide a valuable habitat for birds.

ABOVE LEFT: A pair of blue duck. The birds' preferred location is in high country fast flowing rivers, particularly those bordering forest, but they may also be seen on a few larger, slow-flowing rivers.

ABOVE: The black shag or cormorant is a cosmopolitan species. Subspecies occur in many countries of the world, and in Asian countries they are sometimes harnessed and used for fishing.

ABOVE RIGHT: Matata Lagoon in the Bay of Plenty is home to a variety of wetland bird species. The surrounding vegetation harbours bittern, crakes and the secretive fernbird.

BIRDLIFE OF THE WETLANDS

The swift, restless flight of welcome swallows is a common sight as they skim just above the surface of exposed water to collect insects on the wing, or as they circle and wheel high in the sky. Welcome swallows are an Australian species, being first seen in Northland in the mid-1950s where they fed and bred around Lake Omapere. In subsequent years they spread throughout New Zealand, creating their nests of mud, reinforced with grasses, under road-bridges and culverts or in outhouses, cowsheds and sometimes boats. Flying insects are scarce on inland waterways during winter and, at this time, welcome swallows migrate to the milder areas on the coasts, where they can be seen catching flies which have been attracted to flotsam seaweed.

Three species of shag, or cormorant, inhabit freshwater wetlands. Little shags frequently search for fish in very narrow channels separating swamp vegetation, but they also favour slow-moving rivers and the larger lakes. In the breeding season they often associate with little black shags to nest in colonies in riverbank and lakeside trees.

The large black shag, a cosmopolitan species, is more often found on larger lakes or in tidal harbours. It is a shy bird, having been persecuted by anglers because of its competitive fish-feeding habits.

Another conspicuous bird seen in swamps and on riverbanks is the pukeko. Its favourite nesting sites are secluded in clumps of rushes or within tall beds of raupo, but it also feeds on open country and farm pastures.

Kingfishers settle in a variety of habitats. Although sometimes forest-dwelling birds, they are most likely to be found near water and are a common sight on the shores of many lakes, riverbanks and swampland. They choose the branch of a tree or stump protruding from the water as a commanding perch from which to dive for fish or insects. Like most birds, they possess acute eyesight. A kingfisher may be seen to suddenly swoop down, skimming at least 90 metres across a lake to pluck a dragonfly from the surface of the water.

It is common to see harriers hovering above the swamp, gliding effortlessly in search of small birds, frogs or carrion. Harriers also use swamp vegetation as communal roosts and usually nest in these locations.

All the species just discussed are the birdlife most likely to be seen in these wetland environments. However, some birds which are quite common are so secretive that they are seldom observed. The spotless crake and the marsh crake are two such species. Both birds are no larger than a blackbird, but have longer legs and short tails. They feed mainly at dawn and dusk along the edges of channels in the swamp, where they search for insects and grubs.

RIGHT: The wary spotless crake usually nests in clumps of cutty grass in raupo swamps.

BELOW: A New Zealand kingfisher diving for fish.

BELOW LEFT: A pukeko on its nest with a newly hatched chick.

The fernbird is a small endemic warbler that lives among swamp vegetation and in raupo beds. It is also found in some areas well away from water, being quite common in flax, scrub and heather in the Tongariro National Park. Fernbirds, of which there are several subspecies living on outlying islands, are very weak fliers. A rare feature of their tails is that the barbs of the tail feathers are disconnected, giving their tails a fern-like appearance. When flushed from a reed bed, they will fly laboriously, with rapid wingbeats, for only a short distance before flopping into cover.

Pied stilts and a few species of ducks frequent wetland habitats, sometimes accompanied by herons and occasionally the shy, wary bittern. Many species of ducks flock together on secluded lakes or ponds for the autumn moult, when the birds are flightless for about three weeks. Flocking in

BELOW: Fernbirds are very weak fliers and seldom appear above the swamp vegetation. The barbs of their tail feathers are disconnected, so that their tails appear fern-like.

remote lakes when they are in this vulnerable state is a protective measure.

The bittern is becoming increasingly scarce, because of the reduction of its favourite wetland shelters. With its admirably cryptic plumage, a bittern standing motionless among rushes, with its bill held skywards, is very often unnoticed. During the breeding season, male bitterns may be heard making 'booming' calls, a sound which can be imitated by blowing across the top of a large bottle.

The valuable wetland habitats, especially swamplands, will probably continue to be exploited or drained for agricultural use. But in some localities, concerned landowners and conservationists are preserving wetlands to attract and provide sanctuary for our endangered wetland birds.

BELOW: The common pied stilt inhabits inland lakes and swamps as well as coastal harbours and estuaries.

FORESTS

Below, a realm with tangled rankness rife,
Aloft, tree columns in victorious grace.

– WILLIAM PEMBER REEVES

HABITATS OF THE FORESTS

In its primeval state, New Zealand's landscape consisted principally of forest, interspersed with tussock grassland, wetlands, and alpine vegetation. Today the evergreen forests range from the kauri forests of Northland to the extensive beech forests of Fiordland. In many regions there is a mix of broadleaf, beech and hardwood trees, while, particularly in the central and south-east areas of the North Island, pristine forests of ancient podocarp trees still exist. Because of New Zealand's isolation, the lowland podocarp forests are considered to be of international significance, as they are most similar to the ancient forests of Gondwanaland.

The early Polynesian and European settlers drastically modified the land, felling trees and burning vegetation to clear the land for agricultural use and to provide timber. Throughout the country today, most of the lowland forests now visible have, at some time, been exploited for their timber. For this purpose the preferred trees were the native conifers like kauri in the northern regions and the podocarps such as rimu, totara, kahikatea, matai and miro elsewhere. There was not the same demand for species of beech and hardwoods (tawa, rewarewa, pukatea and kamahi). However, with the development of the pulp and wood-chip industry, there was increasing pressure to use these hardwoods, especially beech.

Much of this lowland forest is now regenerating, in spite of browsing by possums and in some regions by deer, goats and the feral pigs which destroy regenerating seedlings. This forest regrowth may be very attractive to some species of birds, providing them with a favourable habitat. However, possums pose a particularly serious problem as they are selective feeders, devouring foliage and fruits which form the staple diet of many bird species. Recent monitoring has shown that possums also eat eggs and chicks and even adult nesting birds.

Many delicate varieties of ferns, miniature orchids, mosses and fungi spread across the rich, moist earth of the forest floor, particularly in the older forests. Most New Zealand trees are evergreen, losing only a few leaves at a time throughout the year. Very few are deciduous, with fuchsia, kowhai and some lacebarks being the exceptions.

Unlogged virgin forest still survives in parts of both the North and South Islands, but even these are not in their pristine state, as all have been modified in some way by browsing animals and introduced predators. However, efforts are being made to address this problem. An example is the Otira Gorge, near Arthur's Pass in the South Island, which was decimated by possums approximately 20 years ago. Following predator control, the area is now regenerating, and in late summer the hillsides are crimson with the blooming of southern rata trees.

North Island

In Northland a relentless campaign, led by the late Professor W.R. McGregor, resulted in the preservation of an area of virgin kauri forest which now forms the Waipoua Forest Sanctuary. Other pockets of kauri forest have now also been protected, but these are pitifully small remnants of the majestic mixed kauri and broadleaf forests which once extended across Northland, the Waitakere Ranges and the Coromandel Peninsula.

The lowland podocarp and hardwood forests of the Waikato, Taranaki and Hawke's Bay have now gone, but again, due to efforts by conservationists, remnants of magnificent, dense podocarp forests have been preserved at Pureora, west of Lake Taupo, and at Whirinaki, adjacent to the Urewera National Park. Extensive stands of mixed rainforest, consisting of podocarps, hardwoods and beech, remain in the Ureweras and to the east in the Raukumara Range, as well as in the Tararua Range in the southern North Island.

In the North Island the predominant coastal forest trees are pohutukawa backed by karaka, kohekohe, puriri and nikau palms. All these species are valuable producers of food for nectar and fruit-feeding birds.

PREVIOUS PAGES: Understorey vegetation on Hen Island.

LEFT: A stand of kauri trees on the Coromandel Peninsula. Kauri forests originally covered large areas of Northland, the Waitakere Ranges and the Coromandel.

BELOW: The tracery of a gully tree fern (*Cyathea cunninghami*). These tree ferns favour damp gullies in forests in both main islands.

ABOVE: Bellbird song may be heard at any time of the day and during every month of the year. Their dawn chorus rings with a crescendo of 'silver sound'.

ABOVE RIGHT: Tui, like bellbirds, sip nectar from a wide range of flowers.

LEFT: Large expanses of beech forest cover subalpine areas of the South Island, extending to over 1000 metres above sea level. At this height they become stunted and are gradually replaced by herbfields. Beech forests are also found in the North Island, such as the Tongariro National Park and the Kaimanawa Ranges. Beech trees are uncommon in the north of the North Island.

South Island

Large expanses of unmodified forest survive in the South Island, particularly *Nothofagus* beech species, the evergreen beech of the southern hemisphere. In north-west Nelson, the upper Buller valley, Matakitaki and Maruia areas, continuous tracts of beech forest remain, often extending into subalpine altitudes, while in Fiordland and the south-west, stands of pure beech forest are predominant. The beech forest of New Zealand comprises five species which grow in different regions, according to altitude and soil type (moist or dry).

Mixed podocarp forest still exists through parts of Westland, where the canopy of rainforest is penetrated by tall rimu and kahikatea. This type of forest also once existed in the wetter regions east of the Southern Alps. Today a remnant can be seen in the Peel Forest, where a few large totara trees survive in this reserve.

Although early Maori settlers cleared practically all forest cover from the east coasts of both main islands, a few remnants of coastal forest still exist. In Fiordland, extensive beech forests grow to the water's edge and in the Catlins and on Stewart Island southern rata flourishes, extending close to the shore. In podocarp forests it is common to see rope-like vines of rata clinging to trees, and native passionfruit (kohia) vines as well as the tough supplejack vines climbing up through foliage.

Exotic forests

Exotic pine forests are now a prominent part of New Zealand's forest landscapes. The preferred species for timber production in New Zealand is the radiata pine, which was first introduced from its native California in 1860. However, it was not until 1922 that the first commercial plantings were established, mainly on the North Island's volcanic plateau. In the 1960s commercial planting was accelerated, and today pine plantations thrive in many parts of the country.

The pine forests provide a rich source of insect food for native bird species as well as introduced birds. However, it appears that the presence of pockets of native forest within, or adjacent to, the pine plantations are essential for the year-round survival of native bird species.

BIRDLIFE OF THE FORESTS

Before the arrival of Europeans, with their predators such as cats, rats and mustelids, a very rich fauna existed in all the forests. Early naturalists and explorers were enthralled by the abundant and diverse forms of birdlife, many of them unique. In particular, one of these was the nocturnal kiwi, with its complete absence of wings, its hair-like feathers, weak eyesight and nostrils situated at the tip of a long, probing bill. Some of the bird species common in the forests at that time are now extinct, such as the huia, piopio and bush wren. Others, for instance the kakapo, saddleback and stitchbird, survive only on predator-free offshore islands.

Birds are an essential part of the forest cycle, and many trees and shrubs depend on them for dispersal of their seed, or for the pollination of their flowers. An exception are beech trees. The hard seeds are unpalatable to birds and they disperse only by being washed away after heavy rain. The small seed of many podocarp trees is attached to a tasty, fleshy fruit and when the fruit is consumed by the bird, the undigested seed is voided with the excreta, often at a considerable distance from the donor tree. Tui, bellbirds, kokako and saddlebacks all feed on the smaller fruits. In addition, the nectar-feeders help to pollinate the flowers of a variety of trees and shrubs including those of the kowhai, pohutukawa, rata, fuchsia and flax. Surprisingly, the insignificant tiny clusters of nectar-flowers that grow directly from the main trunk and branches of the kohekohe tree are favoured by bellbirds, as the sugar content of the nectar is higher than in most other flowers. The fruit of this tree is much sought after by kokako, pigeon, parakeets and kaka. The kaka, although important in helping to pollinate some of the nectar-producing flowers, does not help in seed dispersal, as it crushes the seed when eating. It has been recently discovered that the native mistletoe flowers need to be twisted by nectar feeders before they open and are pollinated, an action only performed by bellbirds and tui.

TOP: Titoki fruits provide food for birds.

MIDDLE: The puriri tree is the most important 'food tree' for birds as it provides fruit and nectar-bearing flowers throughout most of the year.

BOTTOM: Kohekohe flowers and fruit emerge from the main trunk of the tree.

RIGHT: Until 1964 the North Island saddleback survived only on Hen Island in the Hauraki Gulf, but it now thrives on several offshore islands.

Some forests appear silent and devoid of life, yet other forests of similar structure support an abundance of birds. The reason for this is unknown, and does not appear to be related to the availability of food, but the presence of predators may be a factor.

Isolated fragments of forest support only a few bird species, and usually these are the smaller birds such as fantails, silvereyes and grey warblers. Research has shown that the number of resident bird species in a particular forest is related to its size.

Larger birds like kaka, kokako and the parakeets cannot survive in isolated forests of less than 2000 hectares in size. Some of the strong fliers, particularly pigeons and kaka, will migrate to other areas of forest to feed on flowering and fruiting trees, in season. Even tui will fly some distance to locate flowering flax, kowhai and pohutukawa.

Tui and bellbirds

Tui and bellbirds tend to feed by moving through the forest wherever there is nectar or fruit. Although rather inconspicuous, and much smaller than the tui, the bellbird has a remarkably powerful voice. It is one of the few species of native birds that sings at intervals throughout the day, and during any month of the year. During James Cook's first voyage to New Zealand on the *Endeavour* Joseph Banks, the botanist, went ashore with a party and heard his first bellbird. He then wrote with delight at being wakened at dawn: '...their voices were certainly the most melodious wild music I have ever heard, almost imitating small bells, but with the most tuneable silver sound imagineable.'

Small insectivorous birds

Many of the smaller insectivorous forest birds favour the lower canopy. Most noticeable is the fantail, a flycatcher which flits about in search of insects. As well, tomtits, grey warblers and silvereyes are often seen in this understorey. But whiteheads and yellowheads prefer to feed in the upper canopy.

TOP LEFT: After fledging, fantail chicks stay together for several days, and are fed with insects, by both parents. When the adult female starts building another nest, the male cares for the chicks.

BOTTOM LEFT: The silvereye is common in forests and scrub, often visiting suburban gardens in winter. They feed on fruits, nectar and insects.

TOP RIGHT: The whitehead can be found in many North Island forests, but is absent from Northland, apart from some offshore islands.

BOTTOM RIGHT: The yellowhead occurs only in the South Island where it inhabits beech forests. Both these closely related species feed mainly on insects and spiders, but also eat small fruits. Both species are targeted to incubate the egg and rear the young of the long-tailed cuckoo.

Kokako

The North Island kokako lives precariously in extensive tracts of native forest. However, kokako numbers are increasing in many of these areas following predator control, and they also thrive on bird sanctuaries, such as Tiritiri Matangi. The kokako is a bird of ancient lineage, related to the extinct huia. It is a weak flier, often moving through the forest by springing from branch to branch, rather like a squirrel. The bird builds a substantial nest lined with moss, often in trees draped with passionfruit or supplejack vines. As the female does all the incubating, she is vulnerable to predators. In some areas this has resulted in a disproportionate balance in the sexes. The South Island kokako may be extinct, although sightings have occasionally been reported in some South Island forests and on Stewart Island.

BELOW: A kokako feeding scale insects to its chick. The bird inhabits large stands of native forest where it feeds on vegetation, fruit and flowers. Insects are also taken, particularly during nesting, when chicks require extra protein food.

RIGHT: A kokako chick nestles against its parent. The chick's pink wattles change to a blue colour after its first moult.

BELOW: The endangered North Island kokako is known for its melodious song.

Kaka

Kaka, feeding in the upper canopy, may be observed perched on a high branch and will sometimes respond to a loud whistle, uttering a harsh cry as they fly low. They are dependent on mature forest for nesting, as large trees with holes are usually absent from cut-over forest. As kaka are omnivorous, feeding on fruits, foliage, nectar, insects and grubs, they can find suitable food supplies in regenerating forest. But mature forests provide kaka with dead and rotting trees, which are their favourite feeding sites because they contain insects and succulent huhu grubs.

BELOW: The kaka uses its powerful beak to tear off tree bark in search of insects and their larvae. However, they feed mainly on vegetation, fruits and nectar.

Kaka have specific nesting requirements, selecting the dry cavity of a large tree in which to lay their eggs on a bed of dry wood chips. The entrance to the nest holes is often surprisingly small, some being only 5 centimetres in width at the widest point (the length of a matchbox). It has been found that kaka chicks fledge before they are able to fly strongly, and after leaving the nest spend the first two or three days perched close to, or on, the ground, where they are easy targets for predators. As well, stoats frequently enter nesting holes, even killing the incubating female kaka.

BELOW: A kaka at its nesthole in a puriri tree.

TOP: The endemic yellow-crowned parakeet.

RIGHT: A red-crowned parakeet at the entrance to its nest in a tree cavity. The red-crowned parakeet, or kakariki, is common on many offshore islands, but is becoming increasingly uncommon on the mainland. The yellow-crowned parakeet inhabits podocarp and beech forests on the mainland, as well as on offshore islands. Its diet consists of invertebrates in addition to vegetation, whereas the red-crowned parakeet feeds mainly on vegetation and nectar as well as seeds found on the ground. Both species require dry cavities in mature trees in which to nest.

Kakariki

Kakariki, the small, red-crowned and yellow-crowned parakeets, also require large stands of mature native forest for feeding and nesting. The mature trees provide essential nesting cavities as well as the fruits and vegetation they feed on. The red-crowned parakeet is becoming scarce on the mainland, but is still abundant on offshore islands.

New Zealand pigeons

New Zealand pigeons are most important in the seed-dispersal chain. Besides feeding on the smaller fruits of many tree species, they are able to swallow larger fruits such as those of karaka, puriri, miro, titoki and pigeonwood. They also feed on the fruits of vines such as supplejack and kohia, and in this way the seeds are carried to other parts of the forest, away from the donor tree. Pigeons favour the mixed podocarp habitats that provide them with a wealth of fruits and foliage, but they are uncommon in pure beech forest where their food is scarce. These plump, glossy birds may make their presence known by the low whistling sound

LEFT TOP: A New Zealand pigeon at its nest with a five-day-old chick.

LEFT BOTTOM: A pigeon feeding on the fruit of a nikau palm. Fruit passes through the gut, with the undigested seed being deposited some distance from the donor tree. This helps to regenerate the forest.

BELOW: A pigeon feeding its five-week-old chick by regurgitating partly digested fruit.

of their wingbeats, or by noisily feeding in the forest canopy as they dislodge fruits.

Pigeons lay just one egg per clutch and when the chick is about a week old it is left unattended during the day. From observation, it appears that the chick is fed soon after dawn by each parent, and unless it is fed during the night, this would appear to be the only feed the chick receives each 24 hours, although when older it is sometimes fed during the day. In some instances, when food is plentiful, and this first chick is just a few weeks old, a second nest is made with another single egg being laid in it and incubated.

Grey warblers

With only their beaks as tools, birds are able to build their nests, or furnish tree cavities with soft feathers, grasses or hair. Apart from holes and cavities, most birds build varieties of open nests. The exception to this in the New Zealand forest is the tiny grey warbler. This bird builds an intricate domed nest, often hanging from the canopy of a tree's outermost branches, the point of suspension firmly woven round a branch, with the lower part secured at one or more sides to prevent it from swinging. The nest is totally enclosed, and is decorated and strengthened with spiders' silk, thistledown, lichen and sometimes wool or animal hair, then lined

LEFT TOP: A grey warbler peers from her nest while incubating. The hanging nest is copiously lined with feathers.

LEFT BOTTOM: The shining cuckoo lays one egg in individual grey warblers' nests, leaving the warbler to incubate its egg and foster its chick.

ABOVE: A North Island robin. Robins feed on insects, spiders and earth-worms, often frisking the forest floor, where they are in danger of predation.

with a profusion of feathers. These tiny birds are parasitised by the migrant shining cuckoo, which lays eggs in several grey warblers' nests, leaving the tiny birds to incubate its eggs and rear the cuckoo chicks.

Robins

Perhaps the most confiding forest bird is the robin. One is often unaware of its presence as it perches silently close by, watching for food, its dusky grey body blending with the dim forest background. But if leaf litter is disturbed on the forest floor, it will dart down to snatch up invertebrates that are often too small for our eyes to detect.

Kiwi

Kiwi are unlikely to be seen during daylight hours, except on Stewart Island where they often emerge from their burrows on dull days or well before dusk. The rather plaintive calls of the male kiwi can be heard at night in many forested regions, and in the Northland scrub country. The call of the male bird consists of a series of ascending and descending whistles, in contrast to the female's shorter, harsh cry. Kiwi eat a variety of invertebrates, especially cicada nymphs. They locate insects and grubs in the soft earth by smell, then probe for them with their long bills, leaving telltale conical-shaped holes. In season kiwi also eat ripe berries that have fallen to the ground.

BELOW: A North Island brown kiwi. Kiwi numbers have been drastically reduced by predators, particularly stoats. Recovery programmes with intensive predator control are proving successful in certain localities. The larger great spotted kiwi, inhabiting the forests of north-west Nelson and the Paparoa Range, are more capable of protecting themselves, but their chicks are still vulnerable.

Moreporks

Another well-known nocturnal forest bird is the morepork, New Zealand's only surviving native owl. The larger laughing owl is thought to be extinct, having last been reported in the South Island. Although normally a forest dweller, the morepork has adapted to the changed environment and now inhabits parks and farmland, provided that these include clumps of trees suitable for roosting and nesting. During daylight hours moreporks hide themselves in the deep shade of the forest, under tree-fern fronds or beneath clusters of vines. If their roost is discovered by smaller birds, the morepork is harassed by a cacophony of alarm calls until it is forced to seek a more secluded resting place.

BELOW: A morepork at its nest hole with a weta for its chicks. Moreporks nest in cavities of mature trees or under clumps of perching epiphytes. They feed mainly on insects, but also capture mice and small birds.

The morepork usually nests in tree hollows or in cavities under clumps of astelia. When the chicks are young the male does most of the hunting and after dusk the first food is brought to the nest, consisting usually of large prey such as a lizard, mouse or small bird. Subsequent feeds appear to be composed entirely of insects such as moths, beetles, stick insects and weta.

Bush falcons
Another bird not always noticed is the bush falcon. Often associated with the open high country, the bush falcon or New Zealand falcon has adapted to the forest habitat through evolving darker plumage and more rounded wings to facilitate flight through foliage.

Many people tramp in and explore New Zealand's forests. No botanical knowledge is needed to appreciate the massive dimensions of kauri trees when met face to face, nor to experience the impressive grandeur of trees towering from a luxuriant carpet of ferns and fungi in a dense podocarp forest. The sense of tranquillity within the silent depths of a mossy, southern beech forest is not easily forgotten. Of all habitats, only dense forests remain as 'worlds on their own'.

ABOVE: A weka and her chick. Weka inhabit forest margins and scrub, where they feed on invertebrates, seeds and fruits. They also prey on lizards and rob eggs from ground-nesting birds. Weka are flightless and subject to predation by mustelids and feral cats.

LEFT: A New Zealand kingfisher flying to its nest with an earthworm. Kingfishers occupy a wide range of habitats, being most commonly seen around sheltered coasts and wetlands. They may nest in forests, often by boring a tunnel in the trunk of a dead tree.

HIGH COUNTRY

...the solemn peaks but to the stars are known...

– M. ARNOLD

HABITATS OF THE HIGH COUNTRY

New Zealand is a rugged, mountainous land, with nearly half the country consisting of highland, much of it lying above 300 metres in altitude. So high country and mountain ranges dominate the New Zealand landscape, with the most dramatic formations occurring in the Aoraki/Mount Cook National Park. In clear weather, from almost any part of the country it is possible to view varying heights of hill country.

The symmetrical cone of Taranaki, or Mount Egmont as it is still also known, is often clearly visible from the mountains of the central plateau, 130 kilometres away. Hikurangi, sacred to Maori, is the highest mountain in the east of the North Island, with its summit being the first tip of New Zealand to be illuminated by the rising sun.

The highest peaks of the North Island are the three main mountains of the central range. Most mountains of the North Island are of volcanic origin, and Mount Ruapehu, the highest at 2797 metres, is still active, as are its close neighbours, Mounts Ngauruhoe and Tongariro.

PREVIOUS PAGES: Lake Orbell in the Murchison Mountains, named after Dr. Geoffrey Orbell who rediscovered the takahe in this area in 1948.

BELOW: Taranaki rises above the encircling forests of Mount Egmont National Park. Several species of native birds inhabit these forests. Blue duck have recently been liberated in some of the park's turbulent alpine streams.

Close to the eastern foot of the central North Island mountain range is the very distinctive Rangipo Desert, an area once covered by primeval forest. The catastrophic eruption that formed Lake Taupo, around 1800 years ago, incinerated this forest, completely blanketing it in a thick layer of volcanic ash. It is a bleak but impressive landscape, where strong winds frequently stir the light, gravelly soil into dust storms and where only hardy shrubs, scattered clumps of tussock and ground-hugging subalpine plants will grow. Yet in this inhospitable terrain the banded dotterel and a few passerine birds, such as the New Zealand pipit and some finches, find food, and even nest among the scattered vegetation of tussock and grassland.

A small area on the moist western side of Mount Ruapehu was apparently sheltered from volcanic showers, as luxuriant mixed podocarp forest survives here at the foot of the mountain. This provides a rich habitat for many forest birds, including the honeyeaters, pigeons and insectivorous birds.

BELOW: The Waikato River is the longest river in the North Island. Its source is fed from the snows on the eastern side of Mount Ruapehu.

TOP: The New Zealand pipit is seen at high altitudes where it feeds on insects, spiders and other invertebrates. It also eats seeds and fruits, and in coastal locations feeds on sandhoppers.

ABOVE: Banded dotterel usually nest on shingle riverbeds or on rough, stony pastures. They also nest in the inhospitable terrain of the Rangipo Desert.

RIGHT: The Rangipo Desert, on the eastern side of Tongariro National Park.

The Southern Alps are the most spectacular of New Zealand's mountain landscapes. Extending along much of the western side of the South Island, they have been shaped by glaciers and eroded by streams. At their southern end are the dramatic, sheer-sided mountains of Fiordland, formed of deep troughs gouged out by glaciers. Stretching to the north is a chain of bold granite mountains which border the Westland plains, and over to the east are the Inland and Seaward Kaikouras, geologically young, and still rising. One of the species of tube-nosed seabirds, the endemic Hutton's shearwater, nests in burrows high up in the Seaward Kaikoura Ranges. This unique alpine nesting site was not discovered until 1965.

The highest peak of the Southern Alps is Aoraki/Mount Cook, reaching 3700 metres above sea level. Most of the Southern Alps carry substantial snowfields, and when compacted, the snow supplies ice to several large glaciers. In contrast, North Island mountains support comparatively small snowfields and consequently lack glaciers.

Throughout most of the mountain regions, subalpine forests of beech trees grow to the tree line. The altitude of this limit of tree growth varies with climatic conditions, but the limit is generally higher in the North Island and in alpine Marlborough than it is in southern regions. On North Island mountains and the eastern side of the Southern Alps, mountain beech is the commonest subalpine tree species. It occupies a wider range of habitats than any other species of New Zealand tree.

From the lower hill country to the highest altitudes, vegetation grows accordingly. Generally, temperate forests of beech dominate the lower altitudes, leading into mountain cedar and rata. This gives way at higher altitudes to snow tussock, low turfy grasses, hebes, snowberries and herbs. Mosses, ferns and yellow flax flourish where the earth is moist. Spaniards grow at varying altitudes, sometimes along high-country streams.

Towards the upper limits of the tree line, where trees are more exposed to wind and extreme cold, they become progressively more gnarled and stunted. On the upper altitudes, mountain flowers appear and lichen clings to rocks. This transition is often far more complex than just described, varying considerably from one area to another. The western sides of both the North and South Island ranges receive a high rainfall from prevailing moisture-laden winds crossing the Tasman Sea. The result is a luxuriant growth of trees, particularly evident in the Westland rainforests.

LEFT: The endemic Hutton's shearwater, one of the pelagic tube-nosed seabirds, nests high in the Seaward Kaikoura Mountains. The rock platform in the foreground is a favourite feeding site for white-faced herons and some of the smaller migrant waders, such as turnstones and wandering tattlers.

BIRDLIFE OF THE HIGH COUNTRY

Extensive areas of red tussock grasslands cover much of the foothills and valleys east of the Southern Alps. In places the golden-flowered spaniard and herbs shelter within the tussock. In this expansive uplands habitat the native New Zealand pipit, with a constant characteristic flicking of its tail, runs rapidly along the ground, chasing and snapping up insects. The pipit is sometimes mistaken for the similarly coloured skylark. Above the herb-fields flitter finches and dunnocks, and often, much higher, circling the sky soars a falcon. The falcon takes only live prey and its performance when hunting is impressive, as it bolts at high speed to strike its prey in mid-air.

Brown creepers, common in South Island and Stewart Island lowland forest and scrub, are also seen at higher altitudes, searching for insects in subalpine scrub. Tiny rock wrens inhabit areas of tumbled rock and herb fields above the tree line. They are weak fliers and have unusually large feet. During winter, when the rock falls are blanketed in snow, it is thought that rock wrens are able to find shelter in the spaces between rocks and continue to find insect food. New Zealand's smallest bird, the rifleman, is common in subalpine beech forests of both islands. It is an energetic bird, constantly flicking its wings as it spirals around tree trunks in search of insects and spiders.

BELOW LEFT: The rifleman, New Zealand's smallest bird, is more commonly seen in beech forests throughout New Zealand.

BELOW: The tiny rock wren is related to the rifleman, but is only found in South Island mountain regions where it lives among mounds of fallen rocks. They feed on insects and spiders.

RIGHT TOP: An immature falcon. The main population of the endemic New Zealand falcon inhabits the high country east of the Southern Alps. They also inhabit forest areas in Fiordland and forests in the central North Island. Falcons are only rarely seen north of the North Island volcanic plateau.

RIGHT BOTTOM: An adult falcon with chicks at its nest.

ABOVE: The commonly seen South Island pied oystercatcher usually nests on South Island riverbeds, pastures or arable farmland. Some pairs nest in high-country locations.

LEFT: Blue duck inhabit turbulent alpine rivers, especially where the rivers are bordered by vegetation. They feed on a variety of aquatic invertebrates and also eat fruits and insects which fall from the surrounding trees.

Blue ducks are endemic to New Zealand. They were once common on many waterways, but are now restricted to living on fast-flowing, turbulent mountain rivers, particularly those bordered with trees and vegetation. The birds possess a soft flap of tissue at the tip of their bills, which, it is thought, gives protection from damage when they pluck invertebrates and crustaceans from rocks in turbulent water.

Also found at higher altitudes are Canada geese. Although commonly seen in lowland areas, they often nest near the headwaters of rivers on the east of the Southern Alps. Paradise shelducks may inhabit high-altitude regions, but are more usually located in the lowlands. The South Island oystercatcher, the very common wader present in estuaries throughout New Zealand, nests only in the South Island, and sometimes at high altitudes, although more usually in agricultural grasslands, ploughed pastures and shingle riverbeds.

Several species of birds found in lowland habitats during winter move to upland regions in warmer months. Tui, bellbirds, silvereyes and parakeets can all be found in subalpine forests at these times. Other birds nest at surprisingly high altitudes. Black-backed gulls, which are much more readily associated with New Zealand's coastal habitats, have even been found to nest in the high country. In spring they often eat the placentae left by ewes after lambing.

Takahe

In the valleys of the Murchison mountains to the west of Lake Te Anau, the endemic takahe, thought to be extinct, was rediscovered in 1948 by Dr G. Orbell. The takahe's main diet in the mountains is red tussock, with the birds pulling out the stems and eating the succulent tillers. With this rediscovery of the takahe, the world's largest rail, a captive breeding programme commenced and the Department of Conservation was successful in rearing several birds for release in the wild. The takahe introduced to Tiritiri Matangi now breed there, making their own nests, and are at ease with visitors to the island. The wild population now numbers about 140 birds located in the Murchison mountains.

Kea

Several bird species, which are not found in the North Island, live only in the South Island high country. The most conspicuous of these is the kea, or mountain parrot, the only alpine parrot in the world. These highly intelligent and engaging birds, with their bright scarlet underwing plumage, are familiar to trampers and skiers, but often wreak havoc when they tamper with rubber windscreen wipers of parked cars. The kea is endemic to New Zealand and is a protected species.

FAR LEFT: A kea showing its brightly coloured underwing. The related forest parrot, the kaka, also exhibits a similar underwing colouring.

LEFT: After heavy Fiordland rain the sun illuminates the seedhead of a snow tussock.

BELOW LEFT: The kea is the world's only alpine parrot. It is found only in the South Island in mountainous regions, feeding mainly on vegetation, but also taking carrion. Some rogue birds may attack sick or weakly sheep.

BELOW RIGHT: A takahe feeding its chick. Takahe were introduced to the island sanctuary of Tiritiri Matangi where they have successfully bred.

ABOVE: The male kakapo, at night, in his 'booming' bowl, feeds on an apple placed in his bowl before dark.

RIGHT: Looking down Sinbad Valley to Milford Sound, the valley is cloaked in beech forest, which is a habitat for forest birds.

Kakapo

The kakapo, the world's largest parrot, is a nocturnal bird and is flightless, despite possessing well-developed wings. One of the kakapo's last mainland strongholds was in the forest and alpine scrub of Fiordland, where a few male birds may still survive. In this area the tall snow tussock is a favoured kakapo food, with the leaves being chewed to extract the juices, leaving these fibrous, drooping 'chews' as evidence of its presence. The male kakapo occupy territories on high scrub-covered spurs, using a series of bowls connected by carefully manicured tracks. Here at night they repeatedly call out with a deep, resounding boom in an attempt to attract female kakapo. Unfortunately, no females survive in this region, having been eliminated by stoats. This very endangered bird has now been relocated to offshore islands, with the main population living on Codfish Island (Whenua Hou) off the north-west coast of Stewart Island.

ABOVE: The last surviving mainland kakapo were found in the upper Sinbad Valley, seen here to the left of Mitre Peak.

As the popularity and development of some of the mountain areas has increased, access roading to skifields has scarred high country in those areas. As well, much of the original forest cover of the eastern high country has been logged and replaced by tussock and grazing land. However, many of the alpine regions of the western South Island remain relatively unspoiled. The snowcapped mountains and forested hills still form an imposing backdrop to New Zealand's forests, wetlands, open country and the indented coasts which surround them.

URBAN LANDSCAPE

Where the race of men go by...

– S.W. Foss

HABITATS OF THE URBAN LANDSCAPE

Throughout New Zealand, even in remote areas, there is usually some evidence of human development or interference with the natural environments, but in the urban landscape this evidence is total. And it continues, with the bulldozing of hillsides, construction developments and road complexes in the open country which at times reach as far as the forests. Subdivisions creep into the rural landscape, and holiday settlements stretch along a lot of the coastline.

However, there has been much 'greening' to counteract the seeming sterility of the urban environment. Many New Zealand towns and cities boast parklands and flower gardens, and today the progressive development and enhancement of these parks and gardens, along with street beautification, are an integral part of city councils' activities. New Zealanders share an enthusiasm for gardening that helps re-establish some of the natural world to the urban scene. With the growth of plants, shrubs and trees, insects find a home. And insects, nectar-bearing flowers and edible foliage attract a number of birds. Some birds also enjoy an abundance of café crumbs and the seclusion of park ponds within this urban habitat.

ABOVE: Starlings readily accept garden nest boxes but are sometimes evicted by mynas.

RIGHT: Steps lead through a suburban garden to a starling nest box in the background.

PREVIOUS PAGES: Parkland and ponds provide an urban refuge for birds, which adds to their enjoyment for human visitors.

Some New Zealand settlements are near forests or mountains, but a greater number are sited by rivers or the sea. The indented coastline is notable for a number of deep, natural harbours, and these are often encompassed by towns and cities. Auckland, the largest city, straddles an isthmus, with harbours on either side of it. Seabirds are a common sight along the waterfronts, with terns and shags often perching on wharves or sea walls while squawking gulls chase each other and wheel and swoop in short bursts of activity. In small urban bays, oystercatchers and pied stilts may be seen feeding and resting throughout the year.

Some seabirds will also nest in the quiet bays of the harbours. Large colonies of shags nest close to the city in Auckland's Orakei Basin and in Manukau Harbour. Black-backed gulls even find sheltered sites to nest on city buildings. Blue penguins come ashore at night in certain areas, and are occasionally killed by traffic. This hazard exists along the waterfront road around Wellington's eastern bays.

LEFT: Oystercatchers and gulls on the Auckland waterfront. On the city's shores terns, shags and pied stilts are also commonly seen.

BELOW: Gulls are ever-present on waterfronts and harbours and in some city parks.

Rubbish tips and sewage-treatment plants have a necessary place in the urban landscape, and are in most cases sited away from populated areas. They attract rats and a few feral cats which prey on them. But rubbish tips also attract the scavenging black-backed gulls which circle around the belching earthmovers, searching for food scraps. In winter the settlement ponds tempt large flocks of starlings, sparrows, finches and spotted doves where they find seeds in the piles of dry dredgings from these ponds.

As settlers arrived in New Zealand, they planted trees and shrubs from their homeland. Now these exotic, introduced trees thrive more obviously in the urban landscape. Evergreen native trees grow in town gardens and established parks along with introduced deciduous trees. Many exotic trees and shrubs have added to the stock of food sources available to both endemic and introduced birds. This is especially true of prolific nectar-bearing species.

RIGHT: Gulls, sparrows and feral pigeons are the commonest scavengers around parks and eating places.

BELOW: A spotted dove, along with finches and sparrows, feeds on seeds on a dry sludge heap.

LEFT: A grey duck and her ducklings on a small lake in gardens at Queenstown.

BELOW LEFT: Mute swans in a Wanganui park. City ponds provide food for ducks, geese and swans.

BELOW: The reflection from a red boat in the Taupo Marina colours the water for a cavorting mallard.

BIRDLIFE OF THE URBAN LANDSCAPE

A surprising variety of bird species live and nest in city parks and suburban gardens. Even barren city streets and squares are regularly visited by flocks of feral pigeons and sparrows, as they have become used to an abundance of bread crumbs and leftover lunch scraps. Red-billed gulls and starlings also enjoy this supplementary diet. Pukeko wander round many park ponds or on wet, grassy undeveloped verges beside city roadsides. Even white-faced herons may frequent lush suburban parklands. City ponds are home to ducks, geese, swans and shags, and often attract welcome swallows, which skim across the water to catch insects on the wing.

Even within densely populated city centres, private gardens are popular. Whether these are rambling borders or pots of plants in courtyards, they are as familiar and important to humans as the birdlife which frequently visit them. Certain shrubs bearing nectar-filled flowers attract tui, bellbirds and silvereyes. Containers of sugar solution entice these birds, but wasps and bees may also show interest. On moist lawns, thrushes and blackbirds search for earthworms and grubs, as they would do in their country of origin. The ubiquitous sparrows are regular visitors, ever watchful for handfuls of crumbs. Even the plump native pigeon sometimes visits town gardens where it clambers over trees with ripe fruit, especially the nikau and acmena (monkey apple tree).

In midsummer the garden is alive with the sounds of birds and cicadas, and the activities of an abundance of other insects.

...within the summer garden's lingering murmurs
and every busy hum of life unseen, is yet an
idle air, when all seems still, unending.
– Lynnette Moon

ABOVE LEFT: A pair of silvereyes nesting in a garden hedge. After the nesting season silvereyes may be seen in small groups moving rapidly through foliage. They will visit garden bird tables and feeders for bread, fruit, suet and sugar-water.

TOP: Female house sparrow with nest. A cluster of three to six eggs is incubated by both sexes.

ABOVE: The song thrush, like the blackbird, frequently visits suburban gardens to feed on snails and earthworms.

RIGHT: Moreporks often take moths attracted by street lights.

During winter and when the birds have chicks in spring, they visit town gardens more frequently in search of food. At this time silvereyes are common, and particularly favour pecking at lumps of lard or fat provided for them. Starlings also visit, especially if nest boxes have been placed for them. Unfortunately the myna has proved a predator, observing these nest boxes and not uncommonly attacking young starling chicks and dragging them from their nests. Sometimes the mynas then take over the nest box.

A few true forest dwelling birds, such as the morepork, have adapted to visiting town gardens, where they feed on mice, small birds and insects. They are often attracted to the moths which flit around street lights. The call of the kingfisher in spring, with its repeated 'kek-kek-kek', is a familiar sound, as the bird makes contact to establish territory, prior to nesting. Kingfishers may even nest in urban sites, by tunnelling into trunks of Phoenix palms in parks, into clay banks or rotting trees.

BELOW: In a city square, feral pigeons flock to feed on handfuls of breadcrumbs and grain.

High-rise buildings and tall trees provide roosting sites for most of the town-dwelling birds, where they find safety in height. Feral pigeons, in particular, settle along ledges and parapets. Mature, dense trees like Phoenix palms are favourite roosting sites for the 'murmurations' of starlings. In the evening the birds arrive in chattering, swarming flocks, squeezing into the tree hideouts for safety through the night.

The New Zealand urban scene is a young one by world standards, with no town or city being more than 180 years old. Development has been rapid, and continues apace. There is an absence of the mellowed, historically enduring quality typical of the ancient cities and towns of the 'old world'. But, slowly, the urban landscape should mature, and with that, the spirit which New Zealanders contribute to it.

LEFT: Parapets are popular perches for urban-living feral pigeons.

BELOW: Redpoll at their nest in an apple tree in a suburban garden.

BIBLIOGRAPHY

Bull, P.C., Gaze, P.D. and Robertson, C.J.R., eds, *Atlas of Bird Distribution in New Zealand.* Ornithological Society of New Zealand Inc., 1985.

Checklist of the Birds of New Zealand. Ornithological Society of New Zealand. (Convenor E.G. Turbott), Random Century, Auckland, 1990.

Fleming, C.A., *The Geological History of New Zealand and its Life.* Auckland University Press and Oxford University Press, 1980.

Fleming, C.A., in *New Zealand's Nature Heritage* (partworks). Hamlyn, 1974–76.

Gill, Brian, and Moon, Geoff, *New Zealand's Unique Birds.* Reed Publishing (NZ) Ltd, Auckland, 1999.

Haley, Delphine, *Seabirds.* Pacific Search Press, 1984.

Harrison, Peter, *Seabirds.* Croom Helm Ltd and Reed, 1983.

Hayman, Peter, Marchant, John, and Prater, Tony, *Shorebirds,* Croom Helm, 1986.

Heather, Barry and Robertson, Hugh, *The Field Guide to the Birds of New Zealand.* Viking, 1996.

Lindsey, Terence, and Morris, Rod, *Field Guide to New Zealand Wildlife*, Harper Collins (NZ) Ltd, Auckland, 2000.

Miles, Sue and Moon, Geoff, *The River, The Story of the Waikato.* Heinemann, 1983.

Moon, Geoff, *The Birds Around Us.* Heinemann, 1979.

Moon, Geoff, *The Reed Field Guide to New Zealand Birds.* Reed, 1992 & Reprints.

Moon, Geoff, *The Reed Field Guide to New Zealand Wildlife.* Reed, 1994 & Reprints.

Moon, Geoff with Lockley, Ronald, *New Zealand's Birds.* Heinemann, 1982.

Moon, Lynnette, *The Singing Island.* Godwit, 1998.

Morton, J.E. and Miller, M.C., *The New Zealand Seashore.* Collins, 1973.

Poole, A.L. and Adams, N.M., *Trees and Shrubs of New Zealand.* Govt. Printer, 1979.

INDEX

NOTE: numbers in bold type refer to photograph page numbers.

Dust-jacket, front: *Pied stilts (foreground) and waders*
Dust-jacket, back (clockwise from top left): *Blue penguins; pukeko with chick;*
  New Zealand dotterel chicks; kokako
Half-title page: *New Zealand scaup*
Title page: *Bar-tailed godwits*
Contents page: *Black swans*
Pages 6–7: *Fantails at nest*
Page 158: *Variable oystercatchers*
Above: *Oystercatchers*

First published in 2001 by New Holland Publishers (NZ) Ltd
Auckland • Sydney • London • Cape Town

218 Lake Road, Northcote, Auckland, New Zealand
14 Aquatic Drive, Frenchs Forest, NSW 2086, Australia
86 Edgware Road, London, W2 2EA, United Kingdom
80 McKenzie Street, Cape Town 8001, South Africa

Copyright © 2001 in text: Geoff Moon
Copyright © 2001 in photography: Geoff Moon
Copyright © 2001 New Holland Publishers (NZ) Ltd

ISBN: 1 877246 56 5

Managing editor: Renée Lang
Cover design: Dexter Fry
Design: Barbara Nielsen, Stylus
Editor: Brian O'Flaherty

10 9 8 7 6 5 4 3 2 1

Colour reproduction by PICA Colour Separation, Singapore
Printed by Kyodo Printing Co (Singapore) Pte Ltd